1st EDITION

Perspectives on Diseases and Disorders

Childhood Obesity

Jacqueline Langwith
Book Editor

GALE
CENGAGE Learning·

Detroit • New York • San Francisco • New Haven, Conn • Waterville, Maine • London

Elizabeth Des Chenes, *Director, Publishing Solutions*

© 2013 Greenhaven Press, a part of Gale, Cengage Learning

Gale and Greenhaven Press are registered trademarks used herein under license.

For more information, contact:
Greenhaven Press
27500 Drake Rd.
Farmington Hills, MI 48331-3535
Or you can visit our Internet site at gale.cengage.com

For product information and technology assistance, contact us at

Gale Customer Support, 1-800-877-4253
For permission to use material from this text or product, submit all requests online at
www.cengage.com/permissions

Further permissions questions can be e-mailed to permissionrequest@cengage.com

Articles in Greenhaven Press anthologies are often edited for length to meet page requirements. In addition, original titles of these works are changed to clearly present the main thesis and to explicitly indicate the author's opinion. Every effort is made to ensure that Greenhaven Press accurately reflects the original intent of the authors. Every effort has been made to trace the owners of copyrighted material.

Cover image © Jaimie Duplass/Shutterstock.com

LIBRARY OF CONGRESS CATALOGING-IN-PUBLICATION DATA

Childhood obesity / Jacqueline Langwith, book editor.
     p. cm. -- (Perspectives on diseases and disorders)
  Includes bibliographical references and index.
  ISBN 978-0-7377-6350-8 (hardcover)
  1. Obesity in children--United States. 2. Children--Nutrition--United
States. 3. Obesity in children--United States--Prevention. I. Langwith,
Jacqueline.
  RJ399.C6C472 2012
  618.92'398--dc23
                                                          2012024693

Printed in the United States of America
  2 3 4 5 6 7 16 15 14 13

CONTENTS

A pediatrician reminisces about how childhood obesity has grown from a topic that received little attention in the 1970s to a part of a pediatrician's routine clinical experience today.

FOREWORD

"Medicine, to produce health, has to examine disease."
—Plutarch

Independent research on a health issue is often the first step to complement discussions with a physician. But locating accurate, well-organized, understandable medical information can be a challenge. A simple Internet search on terms such as "cancer" or "diabetes," for example, returns an intimidating number of results. Sifting through the results can be daunting, particularly when some of the information is inconsistent or even contradictory. The Greenhaven Press series Perspectives on Diseases and Disorders offers a solution to the often overwhelming nature of researching diseases and disorders.

From the clinical to the personal, titles in the Perspectives on Diseases and Disorders series provide students and other researchers with authoritative, accessible information in unique anthologies that include basic information about the disease or disorder, controversial aspects of diagnosis and treatment, and first-person accounts of those impacted by the disease. The result is a well-rounded combination of primary and secondary sources that, together, provide the reader with a better understanding of the disease or disorder.

Each volume in Perspectives on Diseases and Disorders explores a particular disease or disorder in detail. Material for each volume is carefully selected from a wide range of sources, including encyclopedias, journals, newspapers, nonfiction books, speeches, government documents, pamphlets, organization newsletters, and position papers. Articles in the first chapter provide an authoritative, up-to-date overview that covers symptoms, causes and effects, treatments, cures, and medical advances. The second chapter presents a substantial number of opposing viewpoints on controversial treatments and other current debates relating to the volume topic. The third chapter offers a variety of personal perspectives on the disease or disorder. Patients, doctors, caregivers, and loved ones represent just some of the voices found in this narrative chapter.

Each Perspectives on Diseases and Disorders volume also includes:

- An **annotated table of contents** that provides a brief summary of each article in the volume.

- An **introduction** specific to the volume topic.

- Full-color **charts and graphs** to illustrate key points, concepts, and theories.

- Full-color **photos** that show aspects of the disease or disorder and enhance textual material.

- **"Fast Facts"** that highlight pertinent additional statistics and surprising points.

- A **glossary** providing users with definitions of important terms.

- A **chronology** of important dates relating to the disease or disorder.

- An annotated list of **organizations to contact** for students and other readers seeking additional information.

- A **bibliography** of additional books and periodicals for further research.

- A detailed **subject index** that allows readers to quickly find the information they need.

Whether a student researching a disorder, a patient recently diagnosed with a disease, or an individual who simply wants to learn more about a particular disease or disorder, a reader who turns to Perspectives on Diseases and Disorders will find a wealth of information in each volume that offers not only basic information, but also vigorous debate from multiple perspectives.

INTRODUCTION

"Liquid candy"—that is what the Center for Science in the Public Interest (CSPI) calls soft drinks. At about 150 calories per twelve-ounce can, Coca-Cola, Pepsi, 7UP, Mountain Dew, and other non-diet sodas have about the same number of calories as eight pieces of Starburst candy or six pieces of Twizzlers strawberry licorice. Surprisingly, though, Starburst and Twizzlers are more nutritious: Starburst candy contains vitamin A, and Twizzlers licorice has iron. Soda generally is devoid of vitamins or minerals, providing only sugar and maybe sodium. The CSPI and many health advocates place a large amount of blame for childhood obesity on soda. They believe that soft drink consumption is associated with obesity and that kids may drink soda instead of more nutritious drinks like milk. Many have suggested that the government should levy a special tax on soda, thereby making it more expensive and potentially reducing consumption and reducing obesity. However, the beverage industry and others disagree with this view. They think that singling out soda is not an effective means of reducing childhood obesity.

Those who support taxes on soda say that if kids drank less "liquid candy," childhood obesity would be reduced. In a widely reported study touted by soda-tax proponents, about five hundred middle school children in the Boston area were surveyed for their lifestyle habits and measured for weight characteristics at the beginning of sixth and seventh grade, and then nineteen months later. The results of the study, which were published in the journal *Lancet* in 2001, indicate that for each can or glass of sugared beverage—such as soda—consumed per day, the likelihood of a child's becoming obese increased by 60 percent. In another analysis published in 2007 and also cited by soda-tax proponents, researchers at the Rudd Center for Food Policy and Obesity at Yale University found that soft drink consumption was associated with increased calorie consumption and weight gain; lower intakes of milk, calcium, and other nutrients; and an increased risk of diabetes and other medical problems.

In an article appearing in a 2009 issue of the *New England Journal of Medicine*, Kelly Brownell, director of the Rudd Center, and Thomas Frieden, director of the Centers for Disease Control and Prevention, argue that the government should use the same approach to lower soft drink consumption as was used to reduce tobacco consumption. They say that taxes have been highly effective in reducing tobacco consumption, and data indicate that higher prices would also reduce soda consumption. Brownell and Frieden cite two studies to back up their claim. First, they note a review conducted by the Rudd Center that suggests that for every 10 percent increase in the price of soda, consumption decreases by 7.8 percent. Second, they cite a study published in *Beverage Digest*, a trade industry publication. According to Brownell and Frieden, the *Beverage Digest* reported that when prices of carbonated soft drinks increased by 6.8 percent, sales dropped by 7.8 percent, and as Coca-Cola prices increased by 12 percent, sales dropped by 14.6 percent. In a 2010 *New York Times* article by food writer Mark Bittman, Brownell explained the rationale behind soda taxes. According to Brownell, "what you want is to reverse the fact that healthy food is too expensive and unhealthy food is too cheap, and the soda tax is a start."[1] Michael F. Jacobson, executive director of the CSPI, agrees, writing in the April 2012 issue of *Nutrition Action Healthletter*, "The single most important thing that federal, state, and local governments could do would be to slap a tax on all sugary drinks."[2]

The Center for Science in the Public Interest and many other health advocates place much of the blame for childhood obesity on soft drinks, often referred to as liquid candy. (© Michael Dwyer/ Alamy)

The beverage industry, libertarians, and others think Brownell, Frieden, and Jacobson are wrong and that soda taxes are a bad idea. According to Susan Neely, president of the American Beverage Association, "If you're trying to manage people being overweight you need a variety of behavior changes to achieve energy balance—it can't be done by eliminating one food from the diet."[3]

In a backgrounder published by the Washington Legal Foundation, the Cato Institute's Patrick Basham, along with John Luik from the Democracy Institute, refute soda-tax proponents' claims that such taxes will decrease consumption. They claim that demand for food is insensitive to price increases. They cite a 2010 study published in *Health Affairs* that found that soft drink taxes do not significantly affect levels of consumption or childhood obesity rates. This study found that the most important predictor of soda consumption was increased hours of TV viewing. According to Basham and Luik, soda taxes, or "fat taxes" as they call them, "have perverse and unintended consequences."[4] They point to a study by University of Washington obesity researcher Adam Drewnowski, which found that when prices for soda increase, low-income consumers consume even fewer healthy foods, such as fruits and vegetables, and eat more processed foods. In addition to believing that taxes will not reduce soda consumption or obesity rates, Basham and Luik are against these taxes for more philosophical reasons. They believe such taxes are economically unfair and infringe on individual autonomy.

As the discussion above indicates, soda taxes are a controversial issue, with both those opposed and those in favor citing studies to support their claims. In *Perspectives on Diseases and Disorders: Childhood Obesity*, the contributors examine the causes and effects of childhood obesity, discuss controversial issues surrounding the condition, and provide a glimpse into the lives of people affected by childhood obesity.

Notes

1. Mark Bittman, "Soda: A Sin We Sip Instead of Smoke?," *New York Times*, February 13, 2010. www.nytimes.com/2010/02/14/weekinreview/14bittman.html.
2. Michael F. Jacobson, "Liquid Candy," *CSPI: Nutrition Action Healthletter*, April 2012. www.cspinet.org/nah/pdfs/liquid-candy.pdf.
3. Quoted in Bittman, "Soda."
4. Patrick Basham and John Luik, "Kicking the Soda Can: Hard Truths About Soft Drink Taxes," Washington Legal Foundation, June 4, 2010. www.wlf.org/Upload/legalstudies/legalbackgrounder/6-4-10BashamLuik_LegalBackgrounder.pdf.

CHAPTER 1

Understanding Childhood Obesity

An Overview of Childhood Obesity

Tish Davidson and Margaret Alic

According to health and medical writers Tish Davidson and Margaret Alic, childhood obesity is a serious public health concern. When children between the ages of two and eighteen years regularly consume more calories than they expend, they accumulate excess weight that can lead to increased risks for myriad health conditions, including diabetes, high blood pressure, liver disease, anxiety, and depression. According to Davidson and Alic, poor eating habits and infrequent exercise are the primary causes of childhood obesity, but the disorder can also be caused by medications and genetic disorders. The authors recommend that children have their body mass index calculated beginning at age two and that parents take an active lead in preventing and/ or fighting childhood obesity.

Childhood obesity is a rapidly growing public health problem in the United States. Although childhood obesity is increasing throughout most of the developed world, the problem is growing fastest in the United States. Over the past two decades the number of obese

SOURCE: Tish Davidson and Margaret Alic, "Childhood Obesity," *Gale Encyclopedia of Children's Health: Infancy Through Adolescence,* 1E. Detroit: Gale, 2006. Copyright © 2006 Cengage Learning.

Photo on facing page. One cause of obesity is taking in more calories than the body subsequently burns. (© Gusto/Photo Researchers, Inc.)

children has doubled and the number of obese adolescents has tripled. According to the National Health and Nutrition Examination Survey of 2003–2006, 31.9% of children and teens were overweight and 16.3% were obese. Thus more than 12 million American children are overweight or obese. Other surveys have found a total obesity rate among children and adolescents of 21–24%. Among American adults 32% are obese and 66% are either overweight or obese.

Significant differences exist in obesity rates among children of different races and ethnic groups, mirroring differences in the adult population. Significantly more Mexican-American boys are overweight than non-Hispanic American black or white boys. Significantly more Mexican-American girls and non-Hispanic American black girls are overweight compared with non-Hispanic white girls. Native Americans and Hawaiians also have higher rates of obesity than whites.

Assessing Healthy Weight: The Body Mass Index

Obesity in children over age two is assessed by the body mass index (BMI), which uses weight and height to calculate a healthy weight range. For most children and teens the BMI is an accurate indicator of body fat. It is age- and sex-specific and is often referred to as BMI-for-age. Children between the ages of 2 and 19 are assigned to a percentile based on their BMI. The percentile is a comparison of their weights with those of other children of the same age and gender. For example, if a boy is in the 65th percentile for his age group, 65 out of every 100 children his age weigh less than he does and 35 weigh more. Adult BMIs are interpreted differently. The BMI weight categories for children are:

- underweight: below the 5th percentile
- healthy weight: 5th percentile to below the 85th percentile

- overweight: 85th percentile to below the 95th percentile
- obese: 95th percentile and above

Children in the top 15 percentiles are considered to be at risk for developing health problems because of their weight.

Risk factors for childhood obesity include:

- inherited tendency toward weight gain
- having at least one obese parent
- eating in response to stress, boredom, or loneliness
- poor sleeping habits
- binge-eating disorders
- mental illness

Causes and Symptoms of Childhood Obesity: The Energy Gap

Obesity is caused by taking in more calories than the body uses. This difference is called the "energy gap." A 2006 study done by the Harvard School of Public Health and published in the journal *Pediatrics* found that, on average, American children consume between 110 and 165 more calories than they use every day. Over a 10-year period these extra calories add 10 pounds to their weight. Teens who are already overweight consume an average of 700–1,000 extra calories every day, resulting in a 10-year average of 58 extra pounds.

The causes of this energy gap are related to both increased food intake and decreased energy usage. Causes of increasing food intake include:

- increased consumption of sugary beverages, accompanied by decreased consumption of milk
- more meals eaten away from home
- more super-sized portions, with portions in some fast-food restaurants having almost tripled since the 1970s
- more use of prepared foods in the home

- increased snacking between meals and fewer family meals
- fewer children taking their lunches from home to school
- increasingly poor eating habits such as skipping breakfast and snacking on high-fat, sugary foods
- increased advertising for high-sugar, high-fat foods directed at children

There are various causes of decreased energy output:
- Children spend more time watching television or at computers than in the past.
- School physical-education requirements have decreased. According to the Centers for Disease Control [and Prevention] only 8% of elementary schools, 6.4% of middle schools, and 5.8% of high schools require daily physical-education classes.
- Fewer children walk to school. In 1969 half of all U.S. school children walked or biked to school, including 87% of children living within 1 mile of their school. By 2003 only 15% of children walked or biked to school.
- Elementary schools have eliminated recesses. More than 28% of schools do not provide a regularly scheduled recess for grades 1–5.
- Increasing fear of crime limits children's outdoor activities.
- Growing affluence has increased teenage access to cars over the past 30 years.

In rare cases medical or genetic disorders can cause childhood obesity. For example Prader-Willi syndrome is a genetic disorder that causes an uncontrollable urge to eat. The only way to prevent a child with Prader-Willi disorder from constantly eating is to maintain an environment with no open access to food. Hormonal disorders such as hypothyroidism also can cause obesity. Certain medications such as cortisone and tricyclic antidepres-

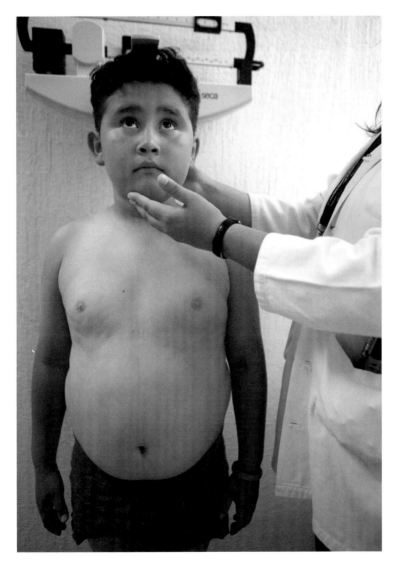

Obesity in children over age two is assessed using the body mass index, which uses weight and height to calculate a healthy weight range. (© **Benedicte Desrus/ Alamy**)

sants may cause weight gain as well. However these are exceptions. Most obese children eat too much and/or exercise too little.

The most obvious symptom of obesity is an accumulation of body fat. Other symptoms involve changes in body chemistry. Some of these changes cause disease in children and others put children at risk for developing health problems later in life. . . .

Diagnosis and Treatment Options

A diagnosis of obesity is usually made based on the child's BMI. The examination will include a family history, medical history, and a complete physical examination.

Tests will include standard blood and urine tests. A thyroid hormone test may be performed to rule out hypothyroidism as the cause of the obesity.

Based on the physician's findings, other tests and procedures may be performed to rule out medical causes of the obesity.

Nutrition education usually involves the entire family. Obese children and their parents are typically referred to a registered dietician or nutritionist who can help them develop a plan for eliminating empty calories and increasing the amounts of nutrient-rich, low-calorie foods in their diets. A nutritionist or dietitian can help families understand how much and what kinds of food are appropriate for their child's age, weight, and activity level. Children may be asked to keep a food diary to record everything that they eat, in order to determine necessary changes in behavior and diet. Obese children are typically encouraged to increase their level of exercise rather than to drastically reduce their caloric intake.

Children who are overweight often have psychological and social problems that can be helped by psychotherapy. Cognitive-behavioral therapy (CBT) is designed to confront and change thoughts and feelings about one's body and behaviors toward food. CBT is relatively short-term and does not address the origins of those thoughts or feelings. CBT may include strategies to maintain self-control with regard to food. Family therapy may help children who overeat for emotional reasons related to conflicts within the family. Family therapy teaches strategies for reducing conflict, disorder, and stress that may be factors in triggering emotional eating.

FAST FACT

According to the Agency for Healthcare Research and Quality, the health care costs of an overweight or obese child are roughly three times higher than those of an average child.

Weight-loss drugs or surgeries are used very rarely in children—only in the most extreme cases of health-threatening obesity after other methods of weight control have failed. However many overweight children suffer from anxiety and depression. Drug therapy to treat these conditions may help children better deal with their obesity and become more involved in physical activities and weight-loss strategies.

Obese teenagers may benefit from structured weight-loss programs such as Weight Watchers or Jenny Craig, with the approval of their physician.

Treatment for childhood obesity begins and ends in the home. Families must make a commitment to following healthy nutritional guidelines, eliminating junk food, sugary drinks, and treats from the home, limiting sedentary activities, and increasing exercise.

Dietary Suggestions for Healthy Children

The American Heart Association adapted the following dietary suggestions for children over age 2 from the federal *Dietary Guidelines for Americans*:

- Children aged 2–3 should obtain no more than 35% of their total calories from fats.
- Children over age 3 should limit their fat intake to about 30% of their total calories. These fats should be monounsaturated or polyunsaturated. Saturated fats and trans fats should be avoided.
- Fruit and vegetable intake should be increased, but fruit juice should be limited.
- At least half of all grains consumed should be whole grains.
- Sugary drinks, such as carbonated soft drinks, should be severely restricted.
- Dairy products should be low-fat or fat-free for children over age 2. Before age 2 children need milk fats for proper growth and development of the nervous system.

- Children should be offered a variety of foods, including fish and shellfish.
- Overfeeding children or making them "clean their plates" should be avoided.

It is often difficult for parents to determine how much food their child should eat at a particular age. However parents tend to overestimate the amount of food that small children require. Active children need more calories and slightly larger amounts of food. The American Heart Association guidelines for daily amounts of some common foods for children of different ages are based on children who are sedentary or physically inactive:

- children aged 2–3 years: total daily calories, 1,000; milk, 2 cups; lean meat or beans, 2 ounces; fruits, 1 cup; vegetables, 1 cup; grains, 3 ounces
- girls aged 4–8 years: total daily calories, 1,200; milk, 2 cups; lean meat or beans, 3 ounces; fruits, 1.5 cups; vegetables, 1 cup; grains, 4 ounces
- boys aged 4–8 years: total daily calories, 1,400; milk, 2 cups; lean meat or beans, 4 ounces; fruits, 1.5 cups; vegetables, 1.5 cups; grains, 5 ounces
- girls aged 9–13 years: total daily calories, 1,600; milk, 3 cups; lean meat or beans, 5 ounces; fruits, 1.5 cups; vegetables, 2 cups; grains, 5 ounces
- boys aged 9–13 years: total daily calories, 1,800; milk, 3 cups; lean meat or beans, 5 ounces; fruits, 1.5 cups; vegetables, 2.5 cups; grains, 6 ounces
- girls aged 14–18 years: total daily calories, 1,800; milk, 3 cups; lean meat or beans, 5 ounces; fruits, 1.5 cups; vegetables, 2.5 cups; grains, 6 ounces
- boys aged 14–18 years: total daily calories, 2,200; milk, 3 cups; lean meat or beans, 6 ounces; fruits, 2 cups; vegetables, 3 cups; grains, 7 ounces

Parents must be very careful in the ways that they approach weight loss with their children. Critical comments about weight from parents or excess zeal in en-

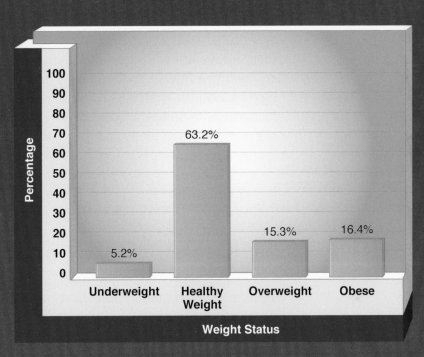

30 Percent of American Children Ages 10–17 Are Overweight or Obese

Weight status of children based on body mass index for age (BMI for age), children age 10–17 only.

Taken from: Data Resource for Child and Adolescent Health, 2007. National Survey of Children's Health, www.childhealthdata.org.

forcing a rigorous diet can trigger eating disorders such as anorexia nervosa or bulimia nervosa in some children, especially adolescent girls.

Prognosis and Prevention

The younger that obese children are when they begin treatment, the better the chances that they will be able to maintain a normal weight. Obese children have an advantage over obese adults in that they are continuing to grow. Obese children that can maintain their weight without gaining may grow into a normal weight as they become taller.

Obese children are at increased risk for:

- type 2 diabetes, which was once seen primarily in older adults but is now being diagnosed in children and young adults at an alarmingly high rate
- high blood pressure (hypertension)
- fat accumulation in the liver (fatty liver/liver disease)
- sleep apnea
- early puberty
- eating disorders
- joint pain
- depression
- anxiety and stress
- low self-esteem
- social prejudice and discrimination

Children who remain obese have a much greater likelihood of becoming obese adults with concomitant health problems. Studies have found that 26–41% of obese preschoolers become obese adults. Among obese school-aged children, 42–63% become obese adults. The greater the degree of obesity, the higher the likelihood that it will continue into adulthood. . . .

Beginning at age two, children and adolescents should have their BMI calculated at each routine physical examination.

Parents must take the lead in preventing childhood obesity. Teaching children to eat a healthy diet sets the framework for lifetime eating habits. Parents should:

- Serve a healthy variety of foods.
- Keep healthy snacks on hand.
- Use low-fat cooking methods such as broiling or baking. Eliminate junk snack food and sugary beverages from the home. This removes temptation and eliminates the need to nag about what not to eat.

- Eat meals together as a family, rather than grabbing food on the run.
- Limit visits to fast-food restaurants.
- Avoid using food as a reward.
- Pack healthy homemade school lunches.
- Encourage school officials to eliminate campus soda machines, bake sales, and fundraisers with candy and cookies.
- Limit television and computer time.
- Plan family activities that involve physical exercise, such as hiking, biking, or swimming.
- Encourage children to become more active in small ways, such as walking to school, biking to friends' houses, or performing chores such as walking the dog or mowing the lawn.
- Set realistic goals for weight control and reward children's efforts.
- Model the eating behaviors and active lifestyle you would like your child [to] adopt.

Childhood Obesity Is a Global Health Concern

Peter Miskin

In the following article Peter Miskin asserts that childhood obesity is a serious public health issue not only in the United States, but around the world. According to Miskin, it is difficult to know precisely how many children around the world are obese or overweight, because there are no universally accepted definitions of the two disorders. However, Miskin says it is clear that a staggering number of children and adolescents in the United States, Europe, and other countries and regions around the world carry excess weight. Miskin believes the myriad detrimental impacts of childhood obesity make it a major global public health concern. Miskin is a nurse and assistant professor at Samuel Merritt University in San Mateo, California.

Childhood obesity is a serious public health issue with a significant long term impact on the population['s] health and cost of healthcare. The primary concern related to childhood obesity stems from the fact that obese children tend to grow into obese adults, with the host of associated health problems. There is a growing concern that if left unchecked, continued growth in the prevalence of childhood overweight and obesity will lead to further increases in the prevalence of adult obesity, which has already reached pandemic proportions.

Evaluating the Global Problem of Childhood Obesity

Even though there is a general consensus that this is one of the most important public health issues, we still do not have universally accepted operating definitions of childhood overweight and obesity. This creates a number of methodological challenges when it comes to evaluation of the scope of the problem. To counter these challenges, the World Health Organization (WHO) has begun developing a set of standardized definitions and tools for nutritional assessment across the lifespan. WHO methodology for the evaluation of nutritional status of children divides all persons under the age of 19 into two age groups: (i) infants and young children under the age of 5, and (ii) school age children and adolescents between the ages of 5 and 19. In 2006, WHO introduced *Child Growth Standards*, which contain standardized body mass index (BMI) tables for the nutritional evaluation of infants and young children under the age of 5. WHO standards for school age children and adolescents are still in development. . . . Adoption of WHO standards may eventually lead towards a set of universally accepted operational definitions of childhood overweight and obesity, which would eliminate the methodological problems that interfere with the evaluation of the problem on the global scale.

Body Mass Index (BMI)

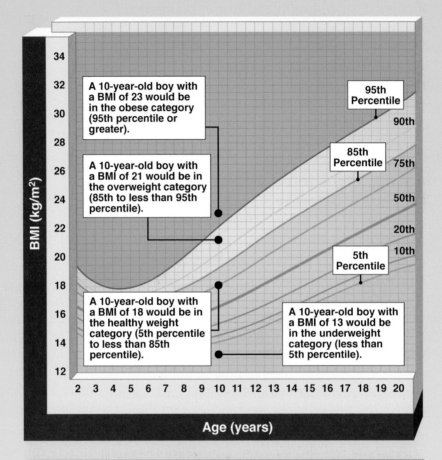

A 10-year-old boy with a BMI of 23 would be in the obese category (95th percentile or greater).

A 10-year-old boy with a BMI of 21 would be in the overweight category (85th to less than 95th percentile).

A 10-year-old boy with a BMI of 18 would be in the healthy weight category (5th percentile to less than 85th percentile).

A 10-year-old boy with a BMI of 13 would be in the underweight category (less than 5th percentile).

95th Percentile
90th
85th Percentile
75th
50th
20th
10th
5th Percentile

BMI (kg/m²)

Age (years)

Weight Status Category	Percentile Range
Underweight	Less than the 5th percentile
Healthy weight	5th percentile to less than the 85th percentile
Overweight	85th to less than the 95th percentile
Obese	Equal to or greater than the 95th percentile

Taken from: US Centers for Disease Control and Prevention, "About BMI for Children and Teens," September 13, 2011. www.cdc.gov.

[The] Centers for Disease Control and Prevention (CDC) also use BMI as a base for the evaluation of nutritional status. However, CDC subscribe to a slightly different approach when it comes to correlating BMI to children's ages. According to CDC (2010), overweight children are the ones whose BMI is between 85th and 95th percentile for the children of the same age and sex. Children whose BMI is above 95th percentile are considered obese. CDC definitions are relatively easy to use, and are frequently utilized in research and literature discussing the problem of childhood obesity.

The lack of universally accepted definitions of overweight and obesity makes the global estimates rather challenging. According to WHO (2010), over 22 million of children under the age of 5 are overweight. The International Obesity Task Force estimated that approximately 10% of children between the ages 5 and 17 are overweight, and up to 3% are obese. This translates into 155 million of overweight, and up to 45 million of obese children worldwide. The WHO (2000) data indicate that overweight and obesity primarily affect populations of the high and high-middle income nations. The global distribution of childhood obesity follows the same pattern.

The epidemiological data for the United States (US) paints a grim picture. In 2007–2008, 9.5% of infants and toddlers in [the] US were at or above the 95th percentile of the BMI for age. In the same period, 11.9% [of] children and adolescents aged 2 through 19 years were at or above the 97th percentile, and 16.9% were at or above the 95th percentile. Moreover, 31.7% of this age group was at or above the 85th percentile.

Other industrialized nations and regions report similar prevalence rates. It has been estimated that 15% of children in Europe are overweight and [an] additional 5% are obese. Similarly high prevalence rates have been

FAST FACT

Globally, nearly 43 million children under the age of five were overweight in 2010, according to the World Health Organization.

reported for some Latin American, North African and Pacific Island nations. Clearly, childhood obesity is a global health problem primarily affecting but not limited to high and middle income nations.

The Impacts of Childhood Obesity

Childhood obesity has been linked to multiple health risks such as blood pressure problems, respiratory abnormalities, dislypidemia, and disturbances of glucose metabolism. For example, increased blood pressure is nine times more common among obese children than among children with normal weight. Obese children are also much more vulnerable to respiratory problems such as asthma, obstructive sleep apnea and pickwickian syndrome [lower oxygen and higher carbon dioxide levels in the blood].

Of a particular concern are the detrimental effects of childhood obesity on metabolism. A study by [B.S.] Freedman, [S.R.] Srinivasan, [D.W.] Harsha, [L.S.] Webber and [G.S.] Berenson (1989) found that overweight and obese children are 2.4 [times] more likely to have elevated total cholesterol, high-density lipoproteins and triglycerides, all of which have been proven to increase the risk of cardiovascular disease. Even more significant is the correlation between childhood obesity and glucose metabolism disturbances. Studies have found that, depending on the age group, up to 25% of the obese children might have impaired glucose tolerance. There is also ample evidence that childhood obesity may lead to a higher prevalence of insulin resistance. Therefore, it does not come as a surprise that the prevalence of type 2 diabetes mellitus among youth in [the] US is on the rise. [The CDC's] SEARCH for Diabetes in Youth Study Group (2006) found the prevalence of type 2 diabetes among youth in [the] US ranging from 0.19 cases per 1000 for non-Hispanic white youth, to 1.74 cases per 1000 for American Indian youth.

Finally, obesity has enormous economic impact. The cost of obesity in [the] US is estimated to be $117 bil-

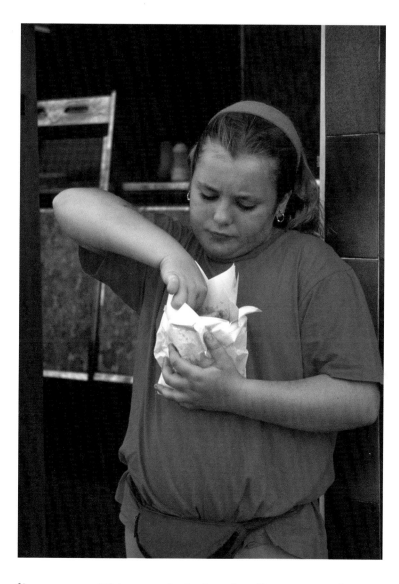

A child in in England eats French fries. Worldwide, approximately 10 percent of children aged five to seventeen are overweight, and 3 percent are obese—about 155 million and 45 million, respectively. (© Bubbles Photolibrary/Alamy)

lion a year. This sum includes the direct cost of treatment and indirect costs associated with loss of work time and productivity. The direct healthcare cost of childhood obesity in [the] US alone is estimated to be $14 billion per annum. The costs of treating problems associated with childhood obesity are continuing to grow. Annual hospital costs were estimated to be $127 million between 1997 and 1999. Compared to the annual costs recorded between 1979 and 1981, this represents [an] increase of $35 million per annum. As the prevalence of childhood obesity continues to grow, it is almost certain that the overall cost of treatment will continue to grow. This will, in turn, drive further increases in the cost of healthcare in the affected regions.

Clearly, the impact of childhood overweight and obesity is too large to be ignored. Current activities of WHO and other national and international health organizations indicate a widespread consensus that is presently one of the most important public health issues. Hopefully, this awareness will translate into a concrete set of measures at multiple levels to address this growing problem. Failure to do so would in [the] long run lead to a dangerous increase in pressure on already strained health resources.

The Health Risks of Childhood Obesity

Susan Levine and Rob Stein

In the following article Susan Levine and Rob Stein document what they assert is a growing burden of childhood obesity. According to the authors, unprecedented numbers of American children are overweight or obese. These children, say Levine and Stein, are too unhealthy to enjoy childhood, are stigmatized, and risk a lifetime of serious diseases and ill health. Childhood obesity threatens the future of the entire nation, say the authors. Levine and Stein are staff writers for the Washington Post.

An epidemic of obesity is compromising the lives of millions of American children, with burgeoning problems that reveal how much more vulnerable young bodies are to the toxic effects of fat.

In ways only beginning to be understood, being overweight at a young age appears to be far more destructive to well-being than adding excess pounds later in life. Virtually every major organ is at risk. The greater damage is probably irreversible.

Doctors are seeing confirmation of this daily: boys and girls in elementary school suffering from high blood pressure, high cholesterol and painful joint conditions; a soaring incidence of type 2 diabetes, once a rarity in pediatricians' offices; even a spike in child gallstones, also once a singularly adult affliction. Minority youth are most severely affected, because so many are pushing the scales into the most dangerous territory.

A Huge Burden of Disease

With one in three children in this country overweight or worse, the future health and productivity of an entire generation—and a nation—could be in jeopardy.

"There's a huge burden of disease that we can anticipate from the growing obesity in kids," said William H. Dietz, director of the Division of Nutrition, Physical Activity and Obesity at the federal Centers for Disease Control and Prevention. "This is a wave that is just moving through the population."

The trouble is a quarter-century of unprecedented growth in girth. Although the rest of the nation is much heavier, too, among those ages 6 to 19 the rate of obesity has not just doubled, as with their parents and grandparents, but has more than tripled.

Because studies indicate that many will never overcome their overweight—up to 80 percent of obese teens become obese adults—experts fear an exponential increase in heart disease, strokes, cancer and other health problems as the children move into their 20s and beyond. The evidence suggests that these conditions could occur decades sooner and could greatly diminish the quality of their lives. Many could find themselves disabled in what otherwise would be their most productive years.

The cumulative effect could be the country's first generation destined to have a shorter life span than its predecessor. A 2005 analysis by a team of scientists forecast a two- to five-year drop in life expectancy unless aggressive action manages to reverse obesity rates. Since then, children have only gotten fatter.

"Five years might be an underestimate," lead author S. Jay Olshansky of the University of Illinois at Chicago acknowledged recently. . . .

The epidemic is expected to add billions of dollars to the U.S. health-care bill. Treating a child with obesity is three times more costly than treating the average child, according to a study by Thomson Reuters. The research company pegged the country's overall expense of care for overweight youth at $14 billion annually. A substantial portion is for hospital services, since those patients go more frequently to the emergency room and are two to three times more likely to be admitted.

Given the ominous trend lines, the study concluded, "demand for ER visits, inpatient hospitalizations and outpatient visits is expected to rise dramatically."

Ultimately, the economic calculations will climb higher. No one has yet looked ahead 30 years to project this group's long-term disability and lost earnings, but based on research on the current workforce, which has shown tens of millions of workdays missed annually, indirect costs will also be enormous.

Childhood obesity is nothing less than "a national catastrophe," acting U.S. Surgeon General Steven Galson has declared. The individual toll is equally tragic. "Many of these kids may never escape the corrosive health, psychosocial and economic costs of their obesity," said Risa Lavizzo-Mourey, president of the Robert Wood Johnson Foundation, which has committed at least $500 million over five years to the problem.

FAST FACT

According to the Centers for Disease Control and Prevention, in a population-based sample of five- to seventeen-year-olds, 70 percent of obese children had at least one risk factor for cardiovascular disease, and 39 percent had two or more.

A Vicious Intergenerational Cycle

The cycle of obesity and disease seems to begin before birth: Women who are overweight are more likely to give birth to bigger babies, who are more likely to become

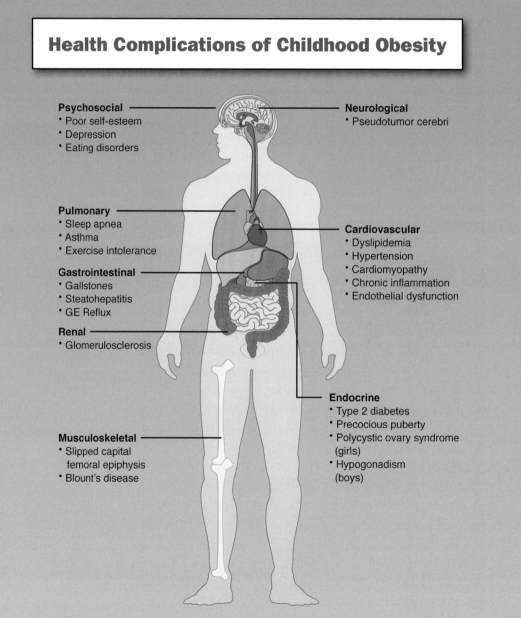

Health Complications of Childhood Obesity

Psychosocial
* Poor self-esteem
* Depression
* Eating disorders

Neurological
* Pseudotumor cerebri

Pulmonary
* Sleep apnea
* Asthma
* Exercise intolerance

Cardiovascular
* Dyslipidemia
* Hypertension
* Cardiomyopathy
* Chronic inflammation
* Endothelial dysfunction

Gastrointestinal
* Gallstones
* Steatohepatitis
* GE Reflux

Renal
* Glomerulosclerosis

Endocrine
* Type 2 diabetes
* Precocious puberty
* Polycystic ovary syndrome (girls)
* Hypogonadism (boys)

Musculoskeletal
* Slipped capital femoral epiphysis
* Blount's disease

Taken from: "The Child with Increasing BMI: A Primer on Pediatric Obesity." University of Wisconsin School of Medicine and Public Health. www.uwhealth.orgpediatric-pathways/pediatric-pathways-a-primer-on-pediatric-obesity/30299.

obese. "And _____ _____ uild it up over generations," said Matthew G_____ _____ professor of ambulatory care and prev____ _____ ____al School. "You get an intergene____ _____ ____ty and disease."

In-utero ex_____ _____ _____edingly complex picture. Patterns _____ _____ ____often set during early childhood, a__ _____ ____rnment and education policies, cultural fa__ _____ __vironmental changes. Income and ethnicity are i__ ____cated, though these days virtually every community has a problem.

In affluent Loudoun County [Virginia], more than a third of 2- to 5-year-olds are overweight. In some lower-income wards in the District [of Columbia], almost half of all schoolchildren and pre-adolescents fit that label. In middle-class Prince George's County [Maryland], nearly a quarter of all children through age 17 are overweight.

The extra pounds appear to weigh more heavily on bodies that are still forming. Fat cells, researchers have found, pump out a host of hormones and other chemicals that might permanently rewire metabolism.

"A child is not just a little adult. They are still developing and changing. Their systems are still in a process of maturing and being fine-tuned," said David S. Ludwig, an obesity expert at Children's Hospital in Boston [Massachusetts]. "Being excessively heavy could distort this natural process of growth and development in ways that irreversibly affect the biological pathways."

As many as 90 percent of overweight children have at least one of a half-dozen avoidable risk factors for heart disease. Even with the most modest increase in future adolescent obesity, a recent study said the United States will face more than 100,000 additional cases of coronary heart disease by 2035.

Lost Childhood

The internal damage does not always take medical testing to diagnose. It is visible as a child laboriously climbs a flight of stairs or tries to sit at a classroom desk, much less rise out of it.

On a playground, obesity exerts a cruel price. "It robs them of their childhood, really," said Melinda S. Sothern of the Louisiana State University Health Sciences Center in New Orleans. "They're robbed of the natural enjoyment of being a kid—being able to play outside, run. If they have high blood pressure, they have a constant risk of stroke."

Physical therapist Brian H. Wrotniak, who works with overweight youth at Children's Hospital of Philadelphia, hears resignation more than anger in his patients' voices. "They complain of simple things like tying their shoes. They can't bend down and tie their shoes because excess fat gets in the way," he said.

An obese boy receives emergency treatment for symptoms related to his weight. Eighty percent of obese teens become obese adults. (© Benedicte Desrus/Alamy)

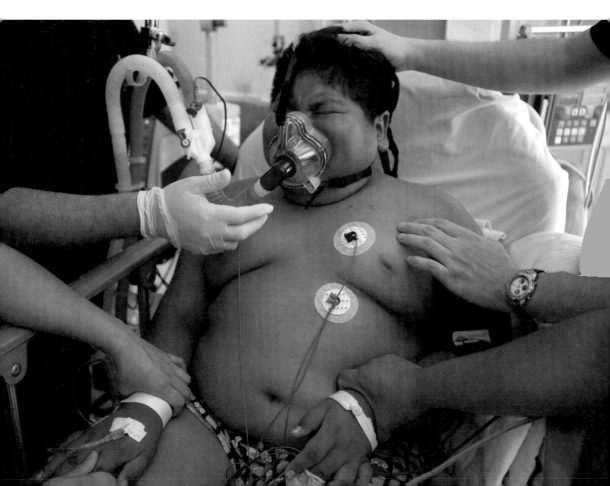

Their Usual Solution: Velcro Sneakers

The emotional distress of these ailments, combined with the social stigma of being fat, makes overweight children prone to psychiatric and behavioral troubles. One analysis found that obese youth were seven times more likely to be depressed.

"Obese children are victimized and bullied," said Jeffrey B. Schwimmer, a pediatric gastroenterologist at the University of California at San Diego and Rady Children's Hospital in San Diego. "Not only do other children treat them differently, but teachers treat them differently. And if you look at obese adolescents, their acceptance into college differs. For obese girls, their socioeconomic status is lower. It cuts a broad swath."

Only within this decade, as studies started to corroborate what doctors were seeing firsthand, has child obesity been recognized as a critical public health concern. For the longest time, the signs were all there, in plain view but largely ignored.

Ludwig compares the situation to global warming.

"We don't have all the data yet, but by the time all the data comes in it's going to be too late," he said. "You don't want to see the water rising on the Potomac [River] before deciding global warming is a problem."

Obese Children Risk Shorter Life Expectancy

Roni Caryn Rabin

In the following article Roni Caryn Rabin discusses a unique study that found that overweight children face a significantly increased risk of dying prematurely compared to their lower-weight peers. The study is unique because it included a large number of children and followed them for decades. The children were from two American Indian communities that had been struggling with obesity even before it became a national public health concern. The study grouped the children based on their body mass index (BMI) and found that children in the group having the highest BMI were more than twice as likely as those with the lowest BMI to die before they reached the age of fifty-five. Rabin is a health writer for the *New York Times*.

A rare study that tracked thousands of children through adulthood found the heaviest youngsters were more than twice as likely as the thinnest to die prematurely, before age 55, of illness or a self-inflicted injury.

Double the Risk of Early Death

Youngsters with a condition called pre-diabetes were at almost double the risk of dying before 55, and those with high blood pressure were at some increased risk. But obesity was the factor most closely associated with an early death, researchers said.

The study, published Thursday [February 11, 2010] in *The New England Journal of Medicine,* analyzed data gathered from Pima and Tohono O'odham Indians, whose rates of obesity and Type 2 diabetes soared decades before weight problems became widespread among other Americans. It is one of the largest studies to have tracked children for several decades after detailed information on weight and risk factors like high cholesterol were gathered.

An American Indian girl participates in an aerobics class on her reservation. Studies of Native Americans have shown that obese children often have shorter life spans than lower-weight children. (© AP Images/ Laura Rauch)

"This suggests," said Helen C. Looker, senior author of the paper and assistant professor of medicine at Mount Sinai Medical Center in New York City, "that obesity in children, even prepubescent children, may have very serious long-term health effects through midlife—that there is something serious being set in motion by obesity at early ages." Dr. Looker added, "We all expect to get beyond 55 these days."

Nearly one in three American children is now considered to be either overweight or obese, and this week [February 2010], the first lady, Michelle Obama, kicked off a campaign intended to end childhood obesity.

The new study analyzed data gathered about 4,857 nondiabetic American Indian children born between 1945 and 1984, when the children were 11 years old on average, and assessed the extent to which body mass index, glucose tolerance, blood pressure and total cholesterol levels predicted premature death.

By 2003, 559 participants had died, including 166 who died of causes other than accidents and homicides, like cardiovascular disease, infections, cancer, diabetes, alcohol poisoning or drug overdose and a large number who died of alcoholic liver disease, which the study's authors suggested might be exacerbated by diabetes.

Adults who had the highest body mass index scores as children were 2.3 times as likely to have died early as those with the lowest scores, and those with the highest glucose levels were 73 percent more likely to have died prematurely.

FAST FACT

According to the World Health Organization, at least 2.8 million people die each year as a result of being overweight or obese.

Child Obesity Warrants Attention

"This really points a finger at impaired glucose tolerance, or pre-diabetes, in ways we have not seen before," said Edward W. Gregg, who is with the diabetes branch of the Centers for Disease Control and Prevention, and [who] wrote an editorial accompanying the article. "We've been aware

Higher Body Mass Index (BMI) Means Higher Incidence of Premature Death

Endogenous causes are those caused by disease or self-inflicted injury. These figures reflect the incidence rate among the affected portion of the population divided by the incidence rate in the unaffected portion of the population.

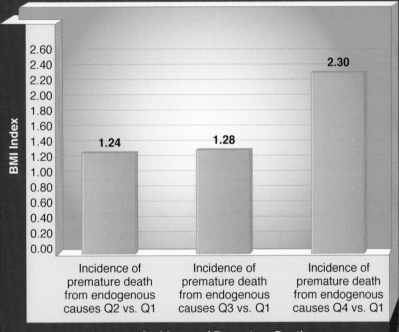

Q1 = Lowest BMI

Q2 = Study participants whose BMI was in the 26% to 50% range

Q3 = Study participants whose BMI was in the 51% to 75% range

Q4 = The 25% of study participants with the highest BMI

Taken from: Paul W. Franks et al. "Childhood Obesity, Other Cardiovascular Risk Factors, and Premature Death." *New England Journal of Medicine*, February 11, 2010.

that pre-diabetes in adults is related to a lot of adverse outcomes, but the relationship in youth has not been as clear. There are not as many long-term studies to document a risk factor like pre-diabetes in youth all the way to adult outcomes."

The study found that high blood pressure in childhood was only a weak predictor of early death and high cholesterol was not associated with premature death, but experts suggested those factors were easier to control with medication.

And though the American Indian community is not representative of the nation's population as a whole, Dr. Gregg said its experience was instructive because "they've tended to be just a decade or two ahead of the rest of the U.S. population" in obesity.

"The message here is that if you take your kid to the doctor and the doctor says, 'Well, their blood pressure is O.K., their cholesterol is O.K. and their sugar's O.K.,' the kid who's obese still warrants our attention," said Dr. Peter F. Belamarich, chief of specialty medicine at the Children's Hospital at Montefiore in the Bronx.

Healthy Environments Can Reduce Childhood Obesity

National Institutes of Health

The National Institutes of Health (NIH), which consists of twenty-seven institutes and centers, is the US government's medical research agency, funding more health research than any other entity in the world. In the following article the NIH discusses the impact children's "built environment" can have on their weight. According to the NIH, a child's home, neighborhood, school, nearby roads, and parks can affect their level of physical activity, how much healthy food they eat, and how much time they spend indoors. The NIH is funding research into the effectiveness of childhood obesity prevention and treatment programs that focus on creating healthy built environments for children.

Kids face a lot of challenges as they grow up: Learning how to make and keep friends, get homework done and have fun while staying safe. But children today are now confronting a growing, oversized problem that puts them at risk for a host of lifelong medical conditions. That problem is childhood obesity.

SOURCE: "Weighty Issues for Kids: Taking Aim at Childhood Obesity," *NIH News in Health*, October 2011.

The National Institutes of Health has found that kids who walk or ride bikes to school are less likely to become obese.

(© Dasha Rosato/Alamy)

Kids won't be able to tackle this one on their own. Fortunately, there's a lot that families and communities can do to help reduce childhood obesity.

Obesity rates have nearly tripled among youth over the past 3 decades. Today, about 1 in 3 children and teens in the U.S. is considered overweight or obese.

Excess weight boosts the chances of developing heart disease, stroke, type 2 diabetes, asthma, liver disease and several types of cancer. Other conditions linked to obesity—such as high blood pressure and high blood cholesterol—are increasingly diagnosed during childhood.

Sadly, medical issues are not the only problems these kids face. Obese children and teens may also struggle with social discrimination, low self-esteem and depression. They are more likely to become obese adults and face continuing troubles.

The main causes of excess weight in childhood are similar to those in adults. Obesity has a strong genetic component, and our in-the-car, computer-bound, food-everywhere society contributes to the problem for an increasing number of people of all ages. But you can help to counteract these influences by creating an environment for your child that encourages healthy eating and physical activity. That effort begins at home.

The Impact of the "Built Environment"

"Adults can help shape the environment that children interact with by providing opportunities to eat healthy food—such as vegetables, fruits and whole grains—and limiting sugar-sweetened beverages and fast food," says Dr. Layla Esposito, who oversees some of NIH's [the National Institutes of Health's] research into childhood obesity. "It's also important to limit screen time on TVs, computers and video games, and provide opportunities for physical activity."

"Newer studies are showing that getting adequate sleep may also be important for weight management," Esposito adds.

Experts agree that our weight is affected by how our environment is structured. Known as the "built environment," it includes not only your home but also everything in your neighborhood and community, including how the roads, parks and food sources are laid out. Experts say built environments don't just affect physical activity; they also affect the foods we choose and how much time we spend inside.

Although it's important for individuals and families to commit to eating healthy and being active, the broader community can also play a role. Kids move among many different environments, all of which shape and affect their decisions about food and activity. Parents, caregivers, schools, governments, community groups and religious organizations can also help by

> **FAST FACT**
>
> According to the 2008 Dietary Guidelines for Americans, published every five years by the US Department of Health and Human Services and the US Department of Agriculture, children and teens need sixty minutes of daily physical activity.

working to develop supportive, healthful environments to encourage these life-long choices.

"I think a lot of people have the sense that it's about willpower and things that are completely in people's control," says Dr. Stephen Daniels, a pediatrician and researcher at the University of Colorado School of Medicine. "If that were the case, we wouldn't have the obesity epidemic that we're having. We live in an environment that is not structured to improve diet and activity choices."

For example, many communities don't have grocery stores, which can mean reduced access to fresh and nutritious foods. In some neighborhoods, the packaged, processed snack foods offered at convenience stores and corner markets are the only choices available.

Some communities don't have safe playgrounds or sidewalks, so children are forced to spend their free time indoors. Sitting instead of moving makes it that much harder to maintain a healthy weight.

The Role of Parents, Schools, and Communities

Among NIH's many ongoing studies in this area are 2 major new research efforts to curb the nation's childhood obesity epidemic. One will evaluate the successes of long-term approaches designed to prevent or treat childhood obesity. The other will examine the efforts communities have been making to reduce childhood obesity.

Rather than focusing only on the behaviors of individuals, these new studies look at existing long-term interventions and consider many different levels of influence, including community youth organizations, schools, home and families.

"The focus is now on multilevel approaches. It's not only the individual, but the family, the physician, schools and the larger community," says NIH's Dr. Charlotte Pratt, who helps manage the new studies. "We have

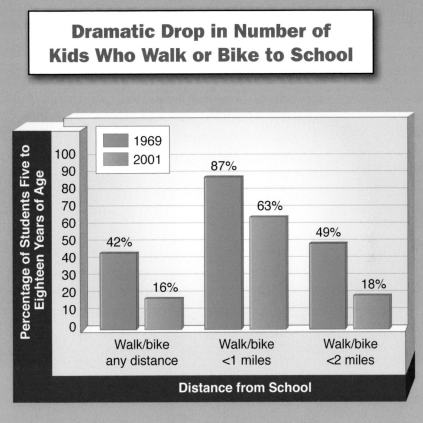

Dramatic Drop in Number of Kids Who Walk or Bike to School

Percentage of Students Five to Eighteen Years of Age

- 1969
- 2001

Walk/bike any distance: 42% (1969), 16% (2001)

Walk/bike <1 miles: 87% (1969), 63% (2001)

Walk/bike <2 miles: 49% (1969), 18% (2001)

Distance from School

Taken from: Centers for Disease Control and Prevention. "Then and Now—Barriers and Solutions," February 25, 2008. www.cdc.gov.

learned of things that work in a single environment, but children do not only live at home."

It's important for parents, teachers, and communities to feel empowered in this fight for the health of a generation and to be role models of healthful behaviors.

"Parents have a really important voice that policymakers need to hear," says Esposito. She encourages parents and communities to consider what they need for change, and then to ask for it. Think about what is being marketed to your kids, if you want more walkable streets or parks, or if you need access to healthier foods or farmer's markets.

You might try making a list of the improvements you could make in your community. Then get together with your neighbors and local leaders to discuss how you can make those ideas a reality. Consider talking to your local school board or PTA [Parent-Teacher Association] about food offerings or advertising in school.

Many communities have started by improving access to and maintenance of local parks; requesting safe and usable bike paths and sidewalks; asking for healthier meals and more physical activity at school; and exploring how to address a lack of nutritious food options and grocery stores.

While you're working to create a healthy environment keep in mind that your own behaviors set a powerful example for your children. If parents aren't making healthy changes and choices for themselves, then it's hard to expect children to understand what's best and make wise choices for themselves.

CHAPTER 2

Controversies Surrounding Childhood Obesity

```
acgctctt ccagctgtcg gacctgggaa attctcctgt gctaaatccc gtggcgc
ggtgtcgc cgcggtgcat cctgggagtt gtagtttttt ctactcagag ggagaat
cagacggg agcaggacgc tgagagaact acatgcagga ggcggggtcc agggcga
ctacgcag cttgcggtgg cgaaggcggc tttagtggca gcatgaagcg caccccg
cgaggaac gagagcgcga agctaagaaa ctgaggcttc ttgaagagct tgaagac
gctccctt atctgacccc caaagatgat gaattctatc agcagtggca gctgaaa
taaactaa ttctccgaga agccagcagt gtatctgagg agctccataa agaggtt
agcctttc tcacactgca caagcatggc tgcttatttc gggacctggt taggatc
caaagatc tgctcactcc ggtatctcgc atcctcattg gtaatccagg ctgcacc
gtacctga acaccaggct ctttacggtc ccctggccag tgaaagggtc taatata
caccgagg ctgaaatagc cgctgcttgt gagaccttcc tcaagctcaa tgactac
gatagaaa ccatccaggc tttggaagaa cttgctgcca aagagaaggc taatgag
tgtgccat tgtgtatgtc tgcagatttc cccaggggttg ggatgggttc atcctac
acaagatg aagtggacat taagagcaga gcagcataca acgtaacttt gctgaat
ggatcctc agaaaatgcc atacctgaaa gaggaacctt attttggcat ggggaaa
agtgagct ggcatcatga tgaaaatctg gtggacaggt cagcggtggc agtgtac
tagctgtg aaggccctga agaggaaagt gaggatgact ctcatctcga aggcagg
tgatattt ggcatgttgg ttttaagatc tcatgggaca tagagacacc tggtttg
accccttc accaaggaga ctgctatttc atgcttgatg atctcaatgc cacccac
ctgtgttt tggccggttc acaacctcgg tttagttcca cccaccgagt ggcagag
aacaggaa ccttggatta tattttacaa cgctgtcagt tggctctgca gaatgtc
cgatgtgg acaatgatga tgtctctttg aaatcctttg agcctgcagt tttgaaa
agaagaaa ttcataatga ggtcgagttt gagtggctga ggcagttttg gtttcaa
tcgataca gaaagtgcac tgactggtgg tgtcaaccca tggctcaact ggaagca
gaagaaga tggagggtgt gacaaatgct gtgcttcatg aagttaaaag agagggg
cgtggaac aaaggaatga aatcttgact gccatccttg cctcgctcac tgcacgc
cctgagga gagaatggca tgccaggtgc cagtcacgaa ttgcccgaac attacct
tcagaagc cagaatgtcg gccatactgg gaaaaggatg atgcttcgat gcctctg
tgacctca cagacatcgt ttcagaactc agaggtcagc ttctggaagc aaaaccc
ggagcaca agtctcaggc ggaggagaaa aagagatcgg cttttctcct ccaacgt
tgggctta agcaagagca gtggagactt ctcttggccc ctagattgta gcacccg
caatccaa aacagctagg aaatggtgcc catgaagttt taaatgtttt aaaatga
tgttatag tctgatttgg tgttaaacag gaccttcttc ccccaaaatt gttcaga
aaatgtga gccattcagc ccccaaggtc cagggcaggc gacaggaacg agcccag
```

Genes Contribute to Childhood Obesity

Office of Public Health Genomics, Centers for Disease Control and Prevention

In the following viewpoint the Office of Public Health Genomics (OPHG) asserts that there is a genetic component to the epidemic of obesity affecting the United States. According to the OPHG, "energy-thrifty genes," which evolved to help humans survive long periods when food was scarce, may be the reason that so many Americans are overweight or obese today. However, energy-thrifty genes may be just a part of the genetic basis of obesity, says the OPHG. It is likely that multiple genes and multiple external factors combine to cause an individual to accumulate excess weight. The Office of Public Health Genomics, within the Centers for Disease Control and Prevention, works to integrate genomics (the study of genes) into public health research, policy, and programs in order to help prevent and control chronic, infectious, environmental, and occupational diseases affecting the US population.

Photo on previous page. The nucleotide sequence of the human FTO gene (pictured) has been implicated in a predisposition to obesity. (© Suzanne Long/Alamy)

SOURCE: "Obesity and Genomics," Office of Public Health Genomics, Centers for Disease Control and Prevention, January 20, 2011.

Obesity results when body fat accumulates over time as a result of a chronic energy imbalance (calories consumed exceed calories expended). Obesity is a major health hazard worldwide and is associated with several relatively common diseases such as diabetes, hypertension, heart disease, and some cancers.

The "Obesity Epidemic" and Genetic Makeup

In recent decades, obesity has reached epidemic proportions in populations whose environments offer an abundance of calorie-rich foods and few opportunities for physical activity. Although changes in the genetic makeup of populations occur too slowly to be responsible for this rapid rise in obesity, genes do play a role in the development of obesity. Most likely, genes regulate how our bodies capture, store, and release energy from food. The origin of these genes, however, might not be recent.

A "Thrifty Genotype" Hypothesis

Any explanation of the obesity epidemic has to include both the role of genetics as well as that of the environment. A commonly quoted genetic explanation for the rapid rise in obesity is the mismatch between today's environment and "energy-thrifty genes" that multiplied in the past under different environmental conditions when food sources were rather unpredictable. In other words, according to the "thrifty genotype" hypothesis, the same genes that helped our ancestors survive occasional famines are now being challenged by environments in which food is plentiful year round.

Other Ways Genes Might Influence Obesity

It has been argued that the thrifty genotype is just part of a wider spectrum of ways in which genes can favor fat accumulation in a given environment. These ways include the drive to overeat (poor regulation of appetite and satiety); the tendency to be sedentary (physically inactive); a diminished ability to use dietary fats as fuel; and an enlarged, easily stimulated capacity to store body fat. Not all people living in industrialized countries with abundant food and reduced physical activity are or will become obese; nor will all obese people have the same body fat distribution or suffer the same health issues. This diversity occurs among groups of the same racial or ethnic background and even within families living in the same environment. The variation in how people respond to the same environmental conditions is an additional indication that genes play a role in the development of obesity. This is consistent with the theory that obesity results from genetic variation interacting with shifting environmental conditions.

FAST FACT

According to the American Academy of Child and Adolescent Psychiatry, if a child has one parent who is obese, there is a 50 percent chance that the child will also be obese. When both parents are obese, the chance increases to 80 percent.

Specific Genes Are Associated with Obesity

The indirect scientific evidence for a genetic basis for obesity comes from a variety of studies. Mostly, this evidence includes studies of resemblance and differences among family members, twins, and adoptees. Another source of evidence includes studies that have found some genes at higher frequencies among the obese (association studies). These investigations suggest that a sizable portion of the weight variation in adults is due to genetic factors. However, identifying these factors has been difficult.

Regarding the direct evidence for obesity genes, the best success stories come from several cases of extreme obesity due to mutations (changes in the genetic material) of single genes (monogenic cases). But those cases account for only a very small fraction of cases worldwide. More recently, however, mutations in a single gene (Melanocortin 4-receptor gene, related to the control of feeding behavior) have been found to be strongly associated with a minority (perhaps 5%) of obesity cases in several populations.

Progress in identifying the multiple genes associated with the most common form of obesity has been slow but is accelerating. As of October 2005 (the latest update of the Human Obesity Gene Map), single mutations in 11 genes were strongly implicated in 176 cases of obesity worldwide. Additionally, 50 chromosomal locations relevant to obesity have been mapped, with potential causal genes identified in most of those regions. (Chromosomes are threadlike structures that contain the genes densely packed into the nucleus of each cell.) Also, studies using genome-wide scans have focused on 253 groups of genes related to obesity, with about one-fifth of them reported by two or more studies. (Genome is the total number of

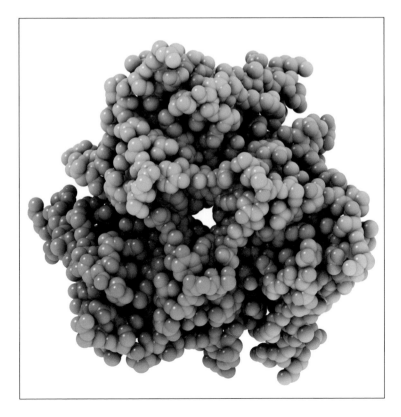

The leptin molecule. Leptin is an appetite-regulating hormone produced by fat tissue. Mutations in the gene that codes for leptin are thought to be responsible for some forms of obesity. (© Laguna Design/Photo Researchers, Inc.)

Identical Twins Are More Likely to Carry the Same Amount of Fat than Nonidentical Twins

The familial occurrences of obesity have been long noted with the concordance for fat mass among MZ (monozygotic, i.e. identical) twins reported to be 70–90 percent, higher than the 35–45 percent concordance in DZ (dizygotic, i.e. fraternal, or nonidentical) twins; as such, the estimated heritability of BMI (body mass index) ranges from 30 to 70 percent.

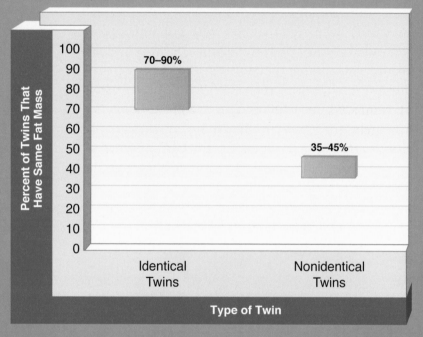

Taken from: Jianhua Zhao and Struan F.A. Grant. "Genetics of Childhood Obesity." *Journal of Obesity*, 2011.

genes contained in the chromosomes.) Finally, 426 variants of 127 genes have been associated with obesity. At least five independent studies have replicated each association in 22 of these genes.

Recently, several independent population-based studies report that a gene of unknown function (FTO, fat mass and obesity-associated gene) might be responsible for up to 22% of all cases of common obesity in the general population. Interestingly, this gene also shows a strong association with diabetes. The mechanism by which this gene operates is currently under intense scientific investigation.

Public Health Genomics Can Help Reduce the Impact of Obesity

Scientists have made great advances in understanding important environmental causes of obesity as well as identifying several of the many genes that might be implicated. Major efforts are now directed toward assessing the interactions of genes and environment in the obesity epidemic. The translation of these efforts into public health practice, from a genomic point of view, will take time.

Fortunately, there is a simple way for public health genomics to start reducing the effects of obesity in populations. It is through the use of family history. Family history reflects genetic susceptibility and environmental exposures shared by close relatives. Health care practitioners can routinely collect family health history to help identify people at high risk of obesity-related disorders such as diabetes, cardiovascular diseases, and some forms of cancer. Weight loss or prevention of excessive weight gains is especially important in this high-risk group. Any health promotion effort to reduce the adverse impact of obesity in populations may be more effective if it directs more intensive lifestyle interventions to high-risk groups (high-risk prevention strategy). However, such strategies should not detract from the population prevention strategy, which recommends that regardless of genetic susceptibility and environmental exposure, all people should follow a healthful diet and incorporate regular physical activity into their daily routine to help reduce the risk of obesity and its associated conditions.

Stress Contributes to Childhood Obesity

Rick Nauert

In the following viewpoint Rick Nauert, senior news editor for the mental health news website Psych Central, asserts that stress is a contributing factor in childhood obesity. According to Nauert, researchers at Iowa State University combed through data collected about children in Boston, Massachusetts; Chicago, Illinois; and San Antonio, Texas, over a period of six years. The data showed that obese children tended to have more stressful events in their lives than nonobese children. According to Nauert, the Iowa State researchers hypothesize that childhood obesity could be caused by biological or behavioral responses to stress.

According to . . . [an] Iowa State University study, increased levels of stress in adolescents are associated with a greater likelihood of them being overweight or obese.

The study of 1,011 adolescents (aged 10–15) and their mothers from low-income families living in three cities—

Boston [Massachusetts], Chicago [Illinois] and San Antonio [Texas]—was posted on the Web site of the *Journal of Adolescent Health*, which will publish it in the August [2009] issue.

Forty-seven percent of the teens in the sample were overweight or obese, but that percentage increased to 56.2 percent among those who were impacted by four or more stressors.

"We found that an adolescent or youth who's more stressed—caused by such things as having poor grades, mental health problems, more aggressive behavior, or doing more drugs and alcohol—is also more likely to be overweight or obese," said lead author Brenda Lohman, an Iowa State assistant professor of human development and family studies (HDFS).

Data Collected from Noted Three-City Study

The study analyzes data obtained from the "Welfare, Children and Families: A Three-City Study"—a six-year longitudinal [repeated observations over a long period of time] investigation. Researchers measured the height and weight of the adolescents to determine their body mass index, which was subsequently used to determine weight status based on two widely used classification systems. Adolescent food insecurity status and individual, maternal and family stressors were also determined through interviews.

The five factors used to determine the individual stressor index for the adolescents were:

- Academic problems
- Consumption of drugs and alcohol
- Depression or poor mental health levels
- Acting out or aggressive behaviors
- Lack of future orientation

The researchers wrote that the adolescents' relationship with stress and becoming overweight may be a result of biological (perturbed hypothalamic-pituitary-adrenal

The stressor index for adolescents includes academic problems, drug and alcohol abuse, depression, aggressive behavior, and a lack of orientation toward the future. (© Janine Wiedel Photolibrary/Alamy)

glands) as well as behavioral responses to stress, such as overeating and lack of exercise.

"It could possibly be that the obesity is leading to these stressors too," Lohman said. "And so the work that we're doing right now looks at which one of these is really coming first: the stressors or the obesity. We know that it is cyclical and that all of these factors just compound on each other."

The study also found that a mother's stress, coupled with food insecurity in the household—a situation in which an individual cannot access enough food to sustain active, healthy living—contributes to a child's chances of becoming overweight or obese.

"In our past research, we did not find this association for older youth (ages 11–17), we only found it for young children (ages 3–10) who were in a house that had enough food or were food-secure," Lohman said.

"But it may be that the adolescents are more cognitively aware of what's going on in the household and they take on their mothers' stress as well. This may be exacerbated in houses where there's not enough food."

Mothers Receive the Initial Focus

While this study singles out mothers, fathers aren't immune to their child's weight status either.

"My own research focuses on fathers and shows that fathers, too, have an effect on children's eating habits and obesity," said [Susan] Stewart, author of the book *Brave New Stepfamilies*, who had another study posted by the *Journal of Adolescent Health* . . . on nonresident father involvement and adolescent eating patterns.

"In our latest study, we found that kids who are involved with nonresident dads eat better—more vegetables, less fast food," she said. "However, similar to the Lohman study, living with a single mom was associated with worse eating habits."

Lohman says the new research should emphasize the need for health care professionals to take a more holistic approach in their treatment of obese teens.

"We absolutely have to focus on their (teens) health, well-being, nutrition and exercise—and education of these things for them," she said. "But we really need to also look holistically at their life and work towards reducing stress and rates of food insecurity for those adolescents as well."

[C. Gundersen], [S.] Garasky and Lohman also published a study out today [May 15, 2009] on the relationship between food insecurity and adolescent obesity. Among 2,516 participants (1,239 girls, 1,277 boys) drawn from the 2001–2004 National Health and Nutrition Examination Survey, 37 percent of families were considered food insecure.

> **FAST FACT**
>
> According to the American Psychological Association, overweight children are more likely to report that their parents were often or always stressed in the previous month.

How Stress Can Contribute to Childhood Obesity

Children who are overweight are more likely than children of normal weight to report eating (27 percent vs. 14 percent) or taking a nap (26 percent vs. 15 percent) to make themselves feel better when they are stressed.

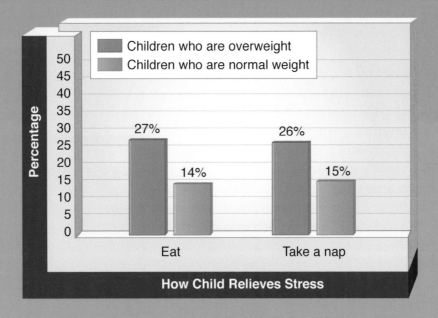

How Do Children Make Themselves Feel Better When They Are Stressed?

Taken from: *American Psychological Association.* "Stress in America 2010; Key Finding." www.stressinamerica.org.

Using five different measures of obesity—BMI [body mass index], waist circumference, triceps skinfold thickness, trunk fat mass, and percent body fat—the researchers determined that 15 to 45 percent of children were classified as obese. Yet they found no statistically significant relationship between food insecurity and obesity, regardless of which indicator was used.

The National Let's Move! Campaign Can Help Reduce Childhood Obesity

Michelle Obama

In the following viewpoint First Lady Michelle Obama talks about the Let's Move! initiative she launched in 2010 to address childhood obesity. Speaking at an elementary school in Philadelphia, Pennsylvania, Obama says the initiative is composed of four parts. The first part seeks to empower parents to make healthy choices for their children. The second part is to provide healthy food in schools. The third part is to increase children's physical activity, and the fourth part is to improve access to healthy, affordable foods in all communities. Obama says that Philadelphia provides an excellent example of the fourth part of the Let's Move! initiative. Many parts of Philadelphia used to be "food deserts," or places devoid of supermarkets and access to fresh foods. However, says Obama, with funding provided by the state of Pennsylvania, more than eighty new supermarkets have been built and are bringing healthy foods to hundreds of thousands of people who formerly lived in a food desert. Obama is an attorney and the wife of the forty-fourth president of the United States, Barack Obama.

SOURCE: Michelle Obama, "Remarks by the First Lady at Fresh Food Financing Initiative," Whitehouse.gov, February 19, 2010.

Six years ago [2004], when this city [Philadelphia, Pennsylvania] had fewer supermarkets per person than almost anywhere in America . . . , when many folks had no access to healthy foods; six years ago many neighborhoods had alarming rates of obesity-related conditions like heart disease and diabetes—the folks in this city, you all could have decided that you had an unsolvable problem on your hands, right? You could have done that. You could have decided that these problems were just too big and too complicated and too entrenched and thrown your hands up and walked away.

But instead you all took a stand, a really important, collaborative stand. You decided first that no family in this city should be spending a fortune on high-priced, low-quality foods because they have no other options. You decided that no child should be consigned to a life of poor health because of what neighborhood his or her family lives in. And you decided that you weren't going to just talk about the problem or wring your hands about the problems, but you were going to act.

And that's precisely the kind of determination, the kind of commitment that we need to address the epidemic of childhood obesity in this country. And this issue is an issue of great concern to me, and I've said this before, not because I'm First Lady—or not just because I'm First Lady of this country—but because I'm a mother, and I care about my kids and I care about all of our kids. And I know that this issue is a great concern to all of you, everyone around this country. We all care about our kids. That's why last week [February 2010] we enthusiastically and proudly launched "Let's Move." "Let's Move" is a nationwide campaign to rally this country around one single but ambitious goal, and that is to end the epidemic of childhood obesity in a generation so that the kids born today grow up with a healthy weight. Simple but ambitious.

So this is what we need to do. Let's move to help families and communities make healthier decisions for their kids. Let's move to bring together our governors and our mayors, our doctors, our nurses, our businesses, our community groups, our parents, teachers, coaches, everyone to tackle this challenge once and for all. And let's move to get our kids what they need to succeed in life. Let's move to ensure that they have the energy and the strength to succeed in school and then in the careers that they choose. Let's move to ensure that they can later live lives where they can keep up with their own kids, maybe keep up with their own grandkids, and if they're blessed, maybe their great-grandkids.

And "Let's Move" is a simple initiative with four parts. . . . First part, let's move to give parents the tools and the information they need to make the healthy choices for their kids. So we're working to provide better labeling for our food and encourage our pediatricians to screen kids for obesity during well-child visits, but then to write a prescription for families when they identify a problem with a step-by-step sort of process for what they can actually do. And we started this wonderful Web site called letsmove.gov to help provide tips and step-by-step strategies on eating well and staying active so parents don't feel alone and isolated as they're trying to figure this out.

Second part: Let's move to get more nutritious food in our schools. [US Agriculture] Secretary [Tom] Vilsack, that's something he's focused on. That's why we're working not just with the Department of Agriculture but with food suppliers, food service workers, school officials, and investing billions of dollars to revamp our school breakfast and lunch programs so that our kids are eating foods with less sugar, fat, and salt, and eating more foods with fresh vegetables and fruits and whole grains.

The third part of the initiative is: Let's move. That's literally let's move. We got to move. We got to find ways

FAST FACT

According to the US Department of Agriculture, French fries are the most common source of vegetable consumed by children and make up one-fourth of children's vegetable intake.

for our kids to be more active, both in and out of school. That's why we're expanding and modernizing the President's Physical Fitness Challenge. And we've recruited professional athletes from all across this country who are just ready and willing to encourage our kids to get and to stay active.

And then finally, one of the reasons why we're here, the final component: Let's move to ensure that all families have access to healthy, affordable food in their own communities. And the approach on this aspect is very simple. We want to replicate your success here in Pennsylvania all across America.

Again, six years ago this state decided to invest $30 million in fresh food financing, which has leveraged $190 million more from the private and non-profit sectors. And so far these investments have funded 83 supermarket projects in 34 counties, bringing nutritious food to more than 400,000 people. And, more importantly in this economy, this investment is projected to create more than 5,000 jobs. And these jobs are occurring often in communities that need them the most. Across this state, right now, because of these efforts, new employees are learning new job skills. . . .

And we saw this example today again during our visit to the Fresh Grocer at Progress Plaza. As you all know, the last supermarket that was in that community closed more than 10 years ago. More than a decade ago. That was the last time that that community had a grocery store. So this community went 10 years without a place for folks to buy good food. For 10 years folks had to buy their groceries at places like convenience stores and gas stations, where usually they don't have a whole lot of fresh food, if any, to choose from. So that means if a mom wanted to buy a head of lettuce to make a salad in this community, or have some fresh fruit for their kids' lunch, that means she would have to get on a bus, navigate public transportation with big bags of groceries, probably more than one

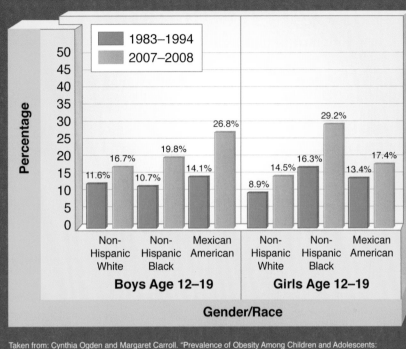

Prevalence of Obesity Among American Teens

Boys Age 12–19

Gender/Race	1983–1994	2007–2008
Non-Hispanic White	11.6%	16.7%
Non-Hispanic Black	10.7%	19.8%
Mexican American	14.1%	26.8%

Girls Age 12–19

Gender/Race	1983–1994	2007–2008
Non-Hispanic White	8.9%	14.5%
Non-Hispanic Black	16.3%	29.2%
Mexican American	13.4%	17.4%

Taken from: Cynthia Ogden and Margaret Carroll. "Prevalence of Obesity Among Children and Adolescents: United States, Trends 1963–1965 Through 2007–2008." *CDC National Center for Health Statistics*, June 2010.

time a week, or, worse yet, pay for a taxicab ride to get to some other supermarket in another community, just to feed her kids.

So let's think about that. For 10 years in one community, there were kids in that community who couldn't get the nutritious food that they needed during some of the most formative years of their lives. And think about the impact that that can have on a child's health, not just now but in the future, because research shows that children who are overweight as adolescents are 70 to 80 percent more likely to become obese as adults.

And what happened in the neighborhood that we visited today is happening somewhere in every state all across this country. Right now there are 23.5 million

Americans, including 6.5 million children, who live in what we call "food deserts." These are places and communities that don't have a supermarket. This is true in the inner city and in rural communities. This is happening all across the country.

But fortunately, right here in Philadelphia, you all have this wonderful grocer named Pat Burns who had already opened successful stores in other neighborhoods. And he decided that it was—he was interested in opening a grocery store in Progress Plaza. And today, just a few months after it opened—and this is important for everybody to understand—the Fresh Grocer is doing a thriving business. It's a beautiful store, attracting folks from neighboring communities and providing jobs for folks in the area. . . .

In Washington, D.C., First Lady Michelle Obama announces the goals of the national Let's Move! campaign to fight childhood obesity, which she launched in 2010. (© Alex Wong/ Getty Images)

So it's because of this example—that part of "Let's Move"—we created this Healthy Food Financing Initiative that's modeled on what's been going on here. And as [US Treasury] Secretary [Timothy] Geithner said, with a modest initial investment of about $400 million a year, we're going to use that money to leverage hundreds of millions more from private and non-profit sectors to bring grocery stores and other healthy food retailers to underserved communities all across this country. If you can do it here, we can do it around the country. And our goal is ambitious. It's to eliminate food deserts in America completely in seven years.

Again, we know this is ambitious, but we also know that tackling the issue of accessibility and affordability is key to achieving the overall goal of solving childhood obesity in this generation. Because we can give our kids the healthiest school breakfasts and lunches imaginable, but that won't mean much if they head to the corner store after school and buy candy and chips and soda because that's all they have available, right? And we can create the best nutrition education and physical education programs in the world, but if dinner is something off of the shelf of a local gas station or convenience store because there's no grocery store nearby, all our best efforts are going to go to waste. We're setting people up for failure if we don't fix this.

So it's clear that we need a comprehensive, coordinated approach. But we also have to be clear that that doesn't mean that it requires a bunch of new laws and policies from Washington, D.C. I have spoken to many experts on this issue, and not a single one of them has said that the solution to this problem is to have government telling people what to do in their own lives.

It's also not about spending huge sums of money, particularly during these times, when so many communities are already stretched thin. Instead, it's about doing more with what we already have.

And as you've shown us here in Philadelphia, it's about smart investments that leverage more investments and then have the potential to pay for themselves many times over in the long run. What you've clearly demonstrated here in this city and in this state is that we can do what's good for our businesses and our economy while doing what's good for our kids and our families and our neighborhoods at the same time. We can do it all.

The Let's Move! Campaign Is an Ill-Conceived Attempt to Address an Imaginary Epidemic

Paul Campos

In the following viewpoint Paul Campos argues that there is no childhood obesity epidemic and that First Lady Michelle Obama's Let's Move! initiative is more harmful than beneficial. According to Campos, before the government should ever get involved in an issue it should, among other things, be reasonably certain that there is an issue to address. He says that Americans in 2011 weigh no more than they did in 2001. The Let's Move! initiative, suggests Campos, is an attempt to get rid of "fat kids." Instead of helping children to become healthier, its focus on losing weight stigmatizes overweight children, he believes.

Campos is a law professor, author, and journalist. His books include *The Obesity Myth*, published in 2004. He writes a weekly column that appears in newspapers around the United States, and he blogs at *Lawyers, Guns and Money*.

SOURCE: Paul Campos, "Michelle Obama's Let's Move Campaign Is Helping Bullies," *The Daily Beast,* March 15, 2011. Copyright © 2011 by The Daily Beast Newsweek. All rights reserved. Reproduced by permission.

Michelle Obama spoke movingly last week [March 10, 2011] at a press conference about how parents agonize over the pain bullies inflict on children. Maybe she should talk to Casey Heynes about that. Heynes is a 16-year-old Australian fat kid who according to his father has been bullied for years by classmates about his weight. . . .

The first lady would, no doubt, be horrified by the suggestion that her Let's Move campaign, which is dedicated to trying to create an America without any fat kids, is itself a particularly invidious form of bullying. But practically speaking, that's exactly what it is. The campaign is in effect arguing that the way to stop the bullying of fat kids is to get rid of fat kids.

Government Activism to Address an Imaginary Epidemic

The whole Let's Move campaign is like a Tea Partier's fever dream of wrongheaded government activism. Now, as a liberal, I believe that government activism is often justified. For more than a generation, this idea has been attacked relentlessly by conservatives, and now the Tea Party movement is subjecting it to fresh assaults. Given our political climate, it's more important than ever for liberals not to assume that a particular government initiative to stop something from happening is a good idea. Rather, we need to be reasonably certain that a) the something in question is actually happening; b) we know why it's happening; c) we know how to stop it from happening; and d) the benefits of stopping it from happening are worth the costs.

Any time liberals support an ambitious government program that fails to meet this test, we are empowering the successors of [former conservative Republican president] Ronald Reagan, who famously declared that "the nine most terrifying words in the English language are 'I'm from the government and I'm here to help.'"

The Let's Move campaign fails this test spectacularly. It has had one notable success, however: According to a Pew Foundation poll, nearly three in five Americans now believe that the government should have "a significant role in reducing childhood obesity."

Predictably, the prevalence of this belief tends to split along partisan lines: 80 percent of liberal Democrats compared to only 37 percent of conservative Republicans and 33 percent of self-described Tea Partiers.

Fat kids have enough problems without government-approved pseudo-scientific garbage about how they could be thin if they just ate their vegetables and played outside more often.

New York Times columnist Charles Blow sees the poll results as evidence that conservatives will oppose anything proposed by Mrs. Obama or her husband [President Barack Obama], "no matter how innocuous or admirable." But there's nothing innocuous or admirable about this crusade. The "childhood obesity epidemic," to the extent that concept ever made any sense, may well be over. As Australian scholar Michael Gard points out in his new book, *The End of the Obesity Epidemic,* over the last decade obesity rates among both adults and children have leveled off or declined all over the world, including in the United States. Contrary to alarmist predictions from just a few years ago that by the middle of this century all Americans would be overweight or obese, the "obesity epidemic" has, for the time being at least, stopped. Americans weigh no more than they did a decade ago.

The fact that Americans did not gain weight in the 2000s merely highlights that we don't know why body mass levels increased in the 1980s and 1990s, or indeed why they remained basically stable in the 1960s and 1970s. We don't know if adults or children consume more calories today than they did forty years ago: Even weakly reliable statistics regarding this question don't exist. Similarly, we don't know if people today are less active than they

Michelle Obama takes part in the ground breaking for a White House garden as part of her Let's Move! campaign. The program has come under attack by some for being just another form of government activism. (© AP Images/ Ron Edmonds)

were a generation ago. Nor do we know if caloric intake and activity levels have changed over the past 10 years, when the "obesity epidemic" apparently ended.

In the face of all this, public health authorities invoke what people always invoke when they don't have any good data: "common sense." They argue that it's just common sense that Americans got fatter in the 1980s and 1990s because they ate more, or were less active, or both. But these are far from the only explanations for weight gain in populations. For instance dieters tend to gain more weight over time than non-dieters, non-smokers gain more weight than smokers, and people generally gain weight as they age. Since the 1960s, smoking rates have plummeted, the median age of the population has gone up by nearly 10 years, and dieting has become much more common. In addition, even if we assume that weight gain in the 1980s and 1990s was caused exclusively by changes in caloric consumption and/or activity levels, it's crucial, from a public policy perspective, to have a good idea what the relative contribution of these factors was. If Americans aren't eating more than they were a generation ago, attempts to get them to eat less are especially likely to fail. But we simply don't know whether this is the case.

Remarkably, debates about whether the government ought to have a role in making American children thinner almost never acknowledge that we have no idea how to do this. Consider the first lady's major policy goals: She wants children to eat a healthy balance of nutritious food, both in their homes and at school, and she advocates various reforms that will make it easier for kids to be physically active. These are laudable goals in themselves, but there is no evidence that achieving them would result in a thinner population. Indeed ambitious, resource-intensive versions of Mrs. Obama's initiatives have been implemented on a smaller scale, for example by the Johns Hopkins University Pathways program, which attempted to improve the diets and increase the activity levels of Native American children in three states, while educating their families about health and nutrition. The program had some success in all these areas, but it produced no weight loss among the children as a group. The same basic results, improved health habits but no weight loss, were obtained in the Child and Adolescent Trial for Cardiovascular Health, a similar program involving thousands of ethnically diverse children in four states. Pursuing comparable initiatives at a national level might be worthwhile—these programs did, after all, result in improved health habits among the children who participated—but there is no reason to think the kinds of reforms Mrs. Obama is advocating will make American children thinner. The perverse result could be that an initiative that might have been judged a success had its primary focus been on producing healthier children will instead end up being used as another example of a failed Big Government program, simply because it did not produce thinner ones.

We Should Help Kids Become Healthier, Not Thinner

For the sake of argument, let's assume there's actually an ongoing childhood obesity epidemic, that we understand what is causing it, and that we know how to stop it. Even assuming all this, does it make sense to try to make American children thinner, as opposed to merely healthier? Why, after all, is such a goal so important in an age of increasingly scarce public health resources? At this point, we need to consider how the concept of "childhood obesity" got defined in the first place. The Centers for Disease Control [and Prevention (CDC)] website offers these definitions of "overweight" and "obesity" in children.

Overweight is defined as a BMI [body mass index] at or above the 85th percentile and lower than the 95th percentile for children of the same age and sex. Obesity is defined as a BMI at or above the 95th percentile for children of the same age and sex.

These definitions raise a couple of obvious questions in a nation that has been bombarded with claims that childhood obesity is skyrocketing. After all, by this standard, aren't exactly 10 percent of children always overweight by definition, while another 5 percent are obese? And what's the justification for these statistical cut-points, anyway?

The definitions were created by an expert committee chaired by William Dietz, a CDC bureaucrat who has made a career out of fomenting fat panic. The committee decided that the cut-points for defining "overweight" and "obesity" in children would be determined by height-weight growth chart statistics drawn from the 1960s and 1970s, when children were smaller and childhood malnutrition was more common. The upshot was that the 95th percentile on those charts a generation ago is about the 80th percentile today—hence, the "childhood obesity epidemic."

These definitions are completely arbitrary. The committee members chose them not on the basis of any demonstrated correlation between the statistical cut-points and increased health risk, but rather because there was no standard definition of overweight and obesity in children, and so they invented one. In other words, the "childhood obesity epidemic" was conjured up by bureaucratic fiat.

The committee did this despite Americans being healthier, by every objective measure, than they've ever been: Life expectancy is at an all-time high, and demographers predict it will continue to climb steadily. This isn't surprising given that mortality rates from the nation's two biggest killers, heart disease and cancer, are at historical lows and keep declining, while infectious diseases are under better control than ever. There's no reason to think that today's children won't be healthier as adults than their parents, just as today their parents are healthier than their own parents were at the same age, continuing a pattern that has prevailed since public health records began to be kept in the 19th century. (Tellingly, 50 years ago government officials were issuing dire warnings that a post–World War II explosion of fatness among both American adults and children was going to cause a public health calamity.)

> **FAST FACT**
>
> The Affordable Care Act passed by the US Congress in 2010 requires that health insurers and employers pay the cost of screening children for obesity and providing them with appropriate counseling.

Shaming Fat Children

And none of this even touches on a subtler and more invidious cost to the Let's Move campaign: the profound

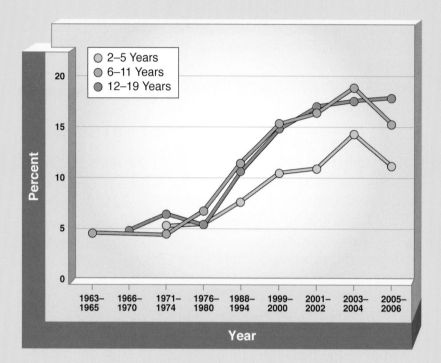

Recent Decrease in Childhood Obesity

Legend:
○ 2–5 Years
◐ 6–11 Years
● 12–19 Years

Overweight is defined as body mass index greater or equal to the gender-and-weight-specific 95th percentile from the 2000 Centers for Disease Control and Prevention Growth Charts.

Taken from: Robert Wood Johnson Foundation. "Childhood Obesity." Robert Wood Johnson Foundation 2008 Annual Report. www.rwjf.org/files/publications/annual/2008/year-in-review/childhood-obesity.html.

shaming and stigmatization of fat children that is an inevitable product of the campaign's absurd premise that the bodies of heavier than average children are by definition defective, and that this "defect" can be cured through lifestyle changes. As Casey Heynes' desperate act of self-defense illustrates [Heynes body slammed the bully, an incident recorded and posted on YouTube], fat kids have enough problems without the additional burden of being subjected to government-approved pseudo-scientific garbage about how they could be thin if they just ate their vegetables and played outside more often.

Michelle Obama's campaign against childhood obesity is exactly the sort of crusade that liberals who don't want to give ammunition to conservative critiques of government activism should oppose. It is a deeply misguided attempt to solve an imaginary health crisis by employing unnecessary cures that in any case don't work. As such, it is almost a parody of activist government at its most clueless. Politically speaking, it deserves the same treatment Heynes gave his tormentors.

Child Health Campaigns That Focus on Fat Are Hate Messages

Marilyn Wann

In the following viewpoint Marilyn Wann contends that government childhood obesity programs such as First Lady Michelle Obama's Let's Move! initiative convey the message that there is something wrong with overweight children. The insidiousness of this message, she says, is reflected in the number of overweight and bullied children who commit suicide. Wann says messages that focus on weight loss are harmful and ineffective and increase the stigma—and the potential bullying—of overweight children. Wann is an author and an activist in the fat acceptance movement. She is the founder of the magazine *Fat!So?* and published a book by the same name in 1998. She is a regular contributor to *SF Weekly*.

The school year has started, which means it's bullying season again for fat children and teens. Fat children in grade school are 63 percent more likely to be teased [than nonfat children], according to a 2010 study published in the American Academy of Pediatrics' journal *Pediatrics*.

SOURCE: Marilyn Wann, "Telling Kids 'Don't Be Fat!' Is a High-Risk Message," *SF Weekly*, September 9, 2011. Copyright © 2011 by SF Weekly. All rights reserved. Reproduced by permission.

The authors seemed surprised by the extent of weight-based bullying.

"What we found, much to our dismay, was that nothing seemed to matter. If you were obese, you were more likely to be bullied, no matter what," said pediatrician Dr. Julie Lumeng.

The federal government is doing its part. President Barack Obama last week [September 2011] declared September to be Childhood Obesity Awareness Month for the second year. On the playground, "awareness" means pointing a finger and shouting, "Hey, fatty!"

The presidential proclamation dovetails with first lady Michelle Obama's Let's Move campaign, which has the goal of "solving the problem of childhood obesity within a generation." (In other words, "No fat chicks—er, children!")

I challenge anyone to name a jurisdiction where weight-loss campaigns have had long-term results, much less done no harm. (A mandatory student weight-loss program in Singapore coincided with a sixfold increase in eating disorders among youth.)

"Don't be fat!" is a high-risk message.

"Bullycide"

Teens who perceive themselves as "too fat"—regardless of what they actually weigh—are more likely to think about suicide and attempt suicide, according to a 2005 study.

In April [2011], two 14-year-old best friends in Minnesota, Haylee Fentress and Paige Moravetz, died in a shared suicide. Haylee was teased for her weight and her red hair. Haylee's aunt, Robin Settle, said that although Haylee wasn't "severely overweight," she was so self-conscious she rarely ate at school.

I first learned about what's now called bullycide among fat youth in 1994.

Brian Head was 15. One day, students were pulling his hair and slapping him. He had been bullied for his weight since seventh grade. He shot himself. In a poem discovered later, Brian described himself, "as an insignificant 'thing,' something to be traded, mangled, and mocked," reports Barbara Colorosa, author of *The Bully, the Bullied and the Bystander.* Brian's father successfully lobbied for a law in Georgia that makes bullying a crime.

I started giving weight diversity talks because of Brian's death. It was scary to go back to the kinds of places where I was teased for being fat and speak against that very thing. (My first talk was to seventh graders in a health education class.) But I found young people of all sizes crave reassurance about bullying and about their appearance.

Brian's death wasn't the last weight-related bullycide. In 1996, I heard about 12-year-old Samuel Graham, who

Marilyn Wann of the National Association to Advance Fat Acceptance says messages that focus on weight loss are harmful and ineffective and increase bullying of overweight children. (© AP Images/Mike Derer)

hanged himself from the family's backyard tree rather than start junior high and face taunts about his weight.

In 1997, English teen Kelly Yeomans was teased for weeks about her weight. She told her family, "It's nothing to do with you. . . . I have had enough and I'm going to take an overdose." [Rock band] Cream bassist Jack Bruce wrote a song, "Kelly's Blues," to try to save other teens via the *Daily Record* newspaper's Save Our Kids appeal in Scotland.

In 2004, eighth-grader April Himes skipped 53 days of school to avoid weight-based bullying. School officials were unable to stop the harassment, but they also informed her she must attend or face a truancy board and possible juvenile detention. At that news, she hanged herself.

Last month [August 2011], a Maryland mother killed her son, Ben Barnhard, and then herself. Her ex-husband speculated that she thought he was better off dead than being bullied again for his weight when the school year started. (News reports say financial and other concerns were also involved.) Ben had appeared on a TV show called *Too Fat for Fifteen* when he attended a weight-loss academy.

In the early 1980s, identical twins Michaela and Samantha Kendall were teased at school for being fat. At age 14, they started dieting to avoid the teasing. They developed anorexia and later died from it.

I hope Malissa Jones escapes their fate. In 2009, when she was 17, she was the youngest person in England to undergo gastric bypass. Media reports labeled her "Britain's fattest teen." In May, they reported she's fighting for her life because of anorexia.

These are just the tragic stories I happen to know about.

Fat children try to defend themselves. Six-year-old LaNiyah Bailey wrote her first book, *Not Fat Because I*

> **FAST FACT**
>
> A study of American middle school students published in the journal *Pediatrics* in 2010 found that obese children have a higher risk of being bullied, regardless of race, socioeconomic status, social skills, academic achievement, or gender.

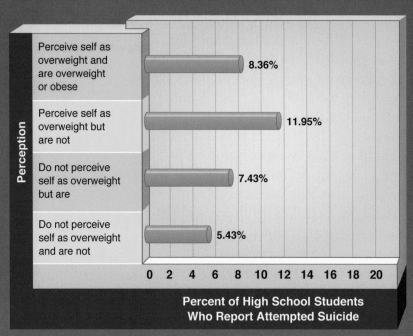

Attempted Suicide and Weight in Adolescents

Overweight is defined here according to the Centers for Disease Control and Prevention (CDC) definition, i.e. body mass index greater than or equal to the 85th percentile. These figures are based on a survey of more than fourteen thousand high school students in 2007.

Taken from: Monica H. Swahn, et. al. Perceived Overweight, BMI, and Risk for Suicide Attempts: Findings from the 2007 Youth Risk Behavior Survey." *Journal of Adolescent Health,* May, 2009.

Wanna Be this year. Her next book is called, *Stand Up! . . . Bully Busters Are Coming to Town.*

Australian teen Casey Heynes suffered weight bullying for years before he fought back and attracted praise from hundreds of thousands of people who saw a videotape of the incident online.

Despite the high risk and impact of bullying on young fat people, the Safe Schools Act of 2010 does not include weight in the list of protected categories. Last month, National Association to Advance Fat Acceptance [NAAFA] leaders held a press conference at the National Press Club asking lawmakers to address this "egregious oversight." NAAFA has created an excellent Child Advocacy Toolkit for people who seek to make schools safe for children of all sizes.

The Right Message Is "Health at Every Size"

Even *National Geographic* last month published on its education website an article promoting Health at Every Size instead of weight-loss goals for youth.

We should not tell fat children that they must change because bullies won't.

If we care about the health and well-being of fat children, we'll protect them from bullies, whether they take individual or institutional form. If we care about the health and well-being of children of all sizes, we'll remove weight stigma and weight-loss goals from nutrition and exercise advice.

"Don't be fat!" is not a health message, it's a hate message.

State Intervention in Life-Threatening Childhood Obesity Is Warranted

Esther J. Cepeda

In the following viewpoint Esther J. Cepeda argues that states should intervene when parents fail to address the severe obesity of their children. Cepeda is bewildered by the "indignant reaction" received by the authors of a medical journal article calling for such intervention. The authors, she notes, call for "level-headed" interventions only in the most extreme cases of childhood obesity. According to Cepeda, government intervention may be needed because parents who do not address their child's obesity are risking the life of their child now and in the future. Cepeda is a nationally syndicated opinion columnist for the Washington Post Writers Group. She also writes weekly columns for the *Chicago Sun-Times*.

Finally, two experts had the courage to state the obvious: Parents who let their children become obese enough to suffer from serious medical complications are committing child abuse.

In their *Journal of the American Medical Association* commentary "State Intervention in Life-Threatening Childhood Obesity," Lindsey Murtagh, a lawyer and research associate at the Harvard School of Public Health, and David S. Ludwig, a doctor for the Optimal Weight for Life Program at Children's Hospital in Boston [Massachusetts], say that despite the well-established right of parents to raise their children as they choose, the state should step into family life in severe cases of life-threatening childhood obesity, just as it would in any other neglect or abuse situation.

Reasonable and Necessary Intervention

Contrary to the worst-case scenarios that flood the mind when you hear someone suggest that obese children need state intervention, the authors did not propose that all parents with overweight kids should have them taken away.

In fact, in their piece they go to great pains to note that for "most of the approximately 2 million children in the United States with a (body mass index) at or beyond

Children today are subject to junk food mass marketing campaigns and are being raised by parents who do not understand proper nutrition, says the author. (© JBP/Alamy)

the 99th percentile . . . state intervention would clearly not be desirable or practical, and probably not be legally justifiable."

They advocate for interventions in the form of in-home social supports, parenting training, counseling and financial assistance, all of which should be offered before resorting to putting an ill child in foster care. But they say such a desperate measure is preferable to letting a child languish under the parents' chronic failure to address a disease with possibly life-threatening and irreversible surgical options, such as bariatric surgery, as a last resort.

Indignant reaction to the authors' level-headed remarks illustrates perfectly the sad state America finds itself in: Our children are not merely overweight but increasingly morbidly obese, and they're pounded by an unending stream of junk-food marketing and being raised by parents who, by and large, don't understand the basic tenets of sound nutrition or exercise. Children are fed cheap, low-quality junk food at school and live in a country where, according to some studies, doctors rarely discuss nutrition with adult patients and are sheepish about telling them they are overweight. Their average neighbor is outraged that in the middle of an obesity epidemic the government wants to label fast food and sugary breakfast cereals as being bad for you.

FAST FACT

All fifty states' child abuse and neglect laws provide that custody may be taken away from parents if they are endangering the welfare of their children.

Murtagh and Ludwig's commentary comes [July 13, 2011] a week after the latest round of startling facts about the scope of this epidemic were released by the Trust for America's Health and the Robert Wood Johnson Foundation in their report "F as in Fat." Nationally, about 16 percent of all children 10 to 17 are not just overweight but obese. Other studies have found that almost 10 percent of infants and toddlers carry excess weight for their length, and slightly more than 20 percent of children between the ages of 2 and 5 are already overweight or obese.

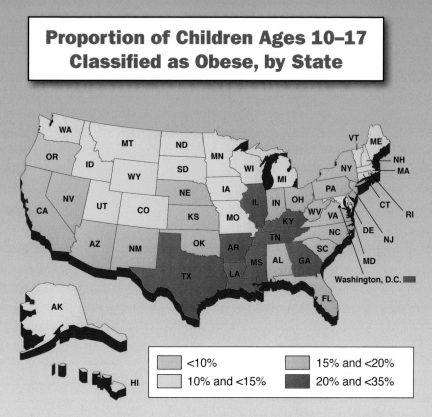

Proportion of Children Ages 10–17 Classified as Obese, by State

Legend:
- <10%
- 10% and <15%
- 15% and <20%
- 20% and <35%

Washington, D.C.

These figures are based on the National Survey on Children's Health, 2007.

Taken from: Trust for America's Health and the Robert Wood Johnson Foundation. *F as in Fat 2011: How Obesity Threatens America's Future,* July 2011.

Have we gotten so numb to these astounding numbers that anyone can seriously question whether letting a child balloon to a life-threatening weight is actual child abuse? Why is this controversial at all?

I spoke to Ludwig to give him a chance to respond to the uniform fury his commentary inspired.

"We were not trying to say we should penalize people for their choices—we live in a very unhealthy environment for children where there is a lot of government inaction on this health issue and little regulation on the practices of [the] food industry," Ludwig said. "This is a hot-button issue at a time where there's a lot of anger at the government and any notion that they could be coming to take away children creates anxiety.

"But the government plays a role in protecting children—that's commonly understood, and no one objects to intervening when there is physical abuse and failure to thrive. We're facing just such a situation with obesity. We have never before seen so many children so massively obese facing not just down-the-road risks, but type 2 diabetes, sleep apnea and actual heart attack collapse immediately resulting from their weight."

By any reasonable measure, children who are living in homes where their lives are at very real risk because their disease is not being well-managed need government intervention—whether it's parenting training, family counseling, financial assistance or foster care. To think otherwise is to write off millions of sick children and the parents who can't, don't know how, or won't take care of them.

State Intervention in Childhood Obesity Would Be Harmful

American Society of Bariatric Physicians

In the following viewpoint the American Society of Bariatric Physicians (ASBP) contends that state intervention, such as the removal of obese children from their homes, is not the proper way to address childhood obesity. According to the ASBP, parents can impact their child's weight. But it is wrong to blame them entirely for a child's weight problem. Removing a child from his or her home will only exacerbate the stress felt by an obese child, who is likely being bullied and discriminated against in most areas of his or her life. The ASBP is a medical professional association for physicians, nurse practitioners, and physician assistants focused on the treatment and management of overweight and obese patients and their related conditions.

The American Society of Bariatric Physicians (ASBP) does not support the concept that state intervention to remove a child from his or her home is the proper way to address life threatening cases of childhood obesity. Comprised of physicians involved in the frontline clinical treatment of obesity, the ASBP believes that in most cases this type of state intervention is extreme and unjustified.

With approximately one out of three children in America considered overweight or obese, it is clear that childhood obesity has reached epidemic proportions. Since the CDC [Centers for Disease Control and Prevention] began tracking childhood obesity data in the mid 1970s, and despite millions of dollars spent on various campaigns and research efforts, childhood obesity rates have continued to rise. ASBP does not attribute this dramatic increase solely to poor parenting.

Race and ethnicity, genetic predisposition, environment in utero and birth weight all affect obesity rates long before any active parenting occurs. After birth, poverty, infant feeding practices, parent education level, and the well recognized cost disparity between healthy and less healthful foods play a role. Children cannot expend energy as in the past due to the unfortunate fear of injury or abduction as well as unsafe sidewalks, trails, and parks left behind due to state budget deficits. In schools, vending machines, poor quality subsidized school lunches, and the regrettable removal of physical education, recess, and health education classes factor in. If that child turns on a computer and browses the internet, she is barraged by cereal, candy, soda and various other unhealthy advertisements. The same occurs if he listens to the radio, downloads music, or turns on the television. Increased caloric density of foods and portion sizes, and introduction of processed foods have also paralleled our obesity epidemic.

FAST FACT

According to the Centers for Disease Control and Prevention, one out of seven low-income preschool-age children are obese.

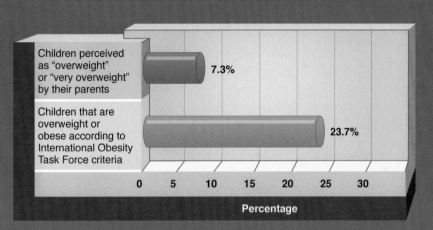

Parents' Perception of Their Children's Weight Is Skewed

Children perceived as "overweight" or "very overweight" by their parents — 7.3%

Children that are overweight or obese according to International Obesity Task Force criteria — 23.7%

Percentage

These figures are based on a study of 536 parents and children in England.

Taken from: A.R. Jones, et al. "Parental Perceptions of Weight Status in Children: The Gateshead Millennium Study." *International Journal of Obesity*, July 2011.

This is not to say that parents are completely defenseless to our obesogenic environment. As physicians who treat childhood obesity, ASBP recognizes that parental involvement is paramount to a child's long term success. Simple changes such as sitting down to dinner as a family, decreasing dining out and fast food consumption, controlling electronics and modeling good behavior can have a significant impact on the weight of the entire family. Parents can drink water instead of sugar sweetened beverages, remove junk foods from the home, decrease processed foods and increase produce (if they can afford to do so and have access to fresh fruits and vegetables). However, these behaviors alone do not guarantee success. Consider an engaged family who has made these changes and the child remains severely obese. ASBP does not agree that the only option is to put him through surgery or remove him from his home.

New York City deputy mayor for health and human services Linda Gibbs speaks to the press about the new law that bans soft drinks of more than sixteen ounces. Critics of government intervention in obesity matters say it is an example of overreach by the government. (© Andrew Burton/ Reuters/Landov)

Approximately two million children are severely obese, clearly more than an overburdened foster care system can handle. Research has shown that the quality of life of an obese child is analogous to that of a child with cancer. Obese children are discriminated against by peers and teachers, and are bullied relentlessly. The additional insult of removing a child from her home will in most cases do more harm than good. In addition, given the fact that $^2/_3$ of our society is overweight and $^1/_3$ obese, the chances that a child will be placed in a home of [a] family who itself struggles with a weight problem is more likely than not.

Choices do exist separate from surgery and state intervention that should be considered, including early recognition and treatment by medical obesity experts. Research has shown that the probability of childhood obesity persisting into adulthood is estimated to be 20% at age four and 80% by adolescence. Research is currently being conducted by bariatricians and other childhood obesity experts using techniques that are much less invasive and equally promising as surgical outcomes without the risks.

Certainly, the premise of turning a severely obese child over to the state is thought provoking, but unless there are clear signs of neglect or abuse in conjunction with the obesity, the ASBP considers it unnecessary, unrealistic and likely damaging to that child long term.

Bariatric Surgery for Children Is Worrisome

Sandy Szwarc

In the following viewpoint Sandy Szwarc argues that the risks, benefits, and long-term impacts of bariatric surgery for children and adolescents are unknown and troubling. She says a study claiming that weight loss surgery can reverse type 2 diabetes in overweight adolescents is flawed and is based more on marketing than it is on research. However, the results of this flawed study have been picked up and sensationalized by the media. According to Szwarc, there is no scientific basis behind the claim that bariatric surgery is safe and effective for children or teens. Szwarc is a registered nurse, researcher, and editorial professional. This piece is part of a series of articles she authored at JunkfoodScience/blogspot.com that examined the medical research, efficacy, and marketing of bariatric surgeries.

R esearch that enables pediatricians to provide the best care for their young patients is something many wonderful doctors truly care about, and certainly parents do, too. That's why it is unimaginable this article appeared in a medical journal. There is simply no credible justification for its publication.

This article [Thomas Inge et al., "Reversal of Type 2 Diabetes Meltitus and Improvements in Cardiovascular Risk Factors After Surgical Weight Loss in Adolescents"] in the January [2009] issue of *Pediatrics*, the journal of the American Academy of Pediatrics, wasn't a clinical trial. In fact, it violated basic principles of medical research and offered no information that any credible healthcare professional would actually use in the care of patients. Its unsupportable conclusions were further sensationalized beyond recognition in a press release, with claims not remotely supported by the findings or the methodology. Yet, it was devoured by gullible journalists and resulted in *331 dramatic news stories* in a single day, with amazing promises that, no doubt, brought countless new customers to the lead medical center.

Sensational News Stories

The headlines have been saying that "Bariatric surgery reverses type 2 diabetes in teens." The media stories have followed the press release issued . . . by Cincinnati Children's Hospital Medical Center. Its tone was similarly breathless, reporting "dramatic, often immediate remission," using the word *dramatic* four times, *remission* five times, and *diabetes-free* twice, along with *breakthrough*, *impressive*, and *significant*. Through a testimonial, claims were made that the surgery resulted in the loss of one-third of body weight and that "remaining diabetes free is well worth" having the surgery.

"Until now," the news release said, "little information was available for families considering surgical weight loss for adolescents." But according to Dr. Thomas Inge, M.D., Ph.D., lead author and surgical director of the teen bariatric program at Cincinnati Children's: "The results have been quite dramatic and to our knowledge, there are no other anti-diabetic therapies that result in more effective and long-term control than that seen with bariatric surgery."

"Dr. Inge and his colleagues agree that the numerous benefits of such procedures will likely outweigh the risks for qualified surgical candidates," it said.

This press release included an obesity epidemic fact sheet from Ethicon-Endo Surgery. Accompanying the print press release, was a video news release by Dr. Inge to explain this "breakthrough study." In it, he also described the "extraordinary results" of a "complete remission" of diabetes and "dramatic reduction" in risks for "heart disease, renal failure and blindness" with "enormous implications for their future health." While there can be complications, these were quickly brushed aside as he said in the same breath, "the real story is that the risks of diabetes may be completely diverted."

According to the authors, bariatric surgeries are critically needed because of rising rates of obesity and type 2 diabetes in children and adolescents. "We previously found a ten-fold increase in the incidence of adolescent type 2 diabetes in Cincinnati from 1982 and 1994," they wrote. (Yes, this is the same Cincinnati Children's Hospital that was the source for the widely repeated fallacy of an epidemic of type 2 diabetes among children and teens.)

But the bariatric study being conducted by these authors has barely begun and is years away from completion. How can long-term effectiveness, extraordinary preventive abilities, and safety have already been shown?

They can't and haven't.

The authors of this study are with the Teen-Longitudinal Assessment of Bariatric Surgery (Teen-LABS) consortium, the five centers with bariatric surgery units awarded a $3.9 million NIH [National Institutes of Health] grant in June 2006. Cincinnati Children's is the coordinating center. Teen-LABS is to be the first-ever study of bariatric surgery on 200 teens to help "determine if it is an appropriate treatment option for extremely overweight teens ... and help them remain at a healthy weight over the long-term." This observational study began enrolling teens in March 2007 and is slated to end in July 2011.

Research or Marketing?

Also linked to the Cincinnati Children's press release page is the brochure for its teen bariatric surgical unit, as well as a *Teen-LABS in the News* section.

How many research studies, purportedly designed to assess the safety and efficacy of a new procedure, have advance publicity featuring before-and-after success stories on *Oprah*, NBC's *Today Show* and various consumer publications? Researchers who set out to objectively answer a scientific question do not use press releases or go on television shows to report the findings years before their study is even completed.

As we've examined, however, the focus of Teen-LABS is less on investigating long-term complications and effects on health (which have previously been identified as concerns by these same investigators), and more about identifying demographic and lifestyle information. . . .

Incredibly, this study in *Pediatrics* wasn't even reporting preliminary data from Teen-LABS. What was it reporting?

A Study That Is Not a Study

This article was a *retrospective* chart review of *eleven* teens who had gastric bypass at the various Teen-LABS bariatric centers between November 2002 and 2004. Select health indices of these teens at one year were compared to those in the electronic medical records of a control group of 53 teens with type 2 diabetes who had been seen at Cincinnati Children's Hospital between 2002 and April 2005. Case reports on a hand-selected group of patients are not the types of studies that doctors can use to evaluate the effectiveness of an intervention and, most importantly, use to weigh the risks and benefits. These are akin to anecdotal evidence.

The first obvious flaw that negates this as a "fair test" of anything is selection bias. Selection bias is like cherry picking. The children chosen to be reported on, after the fact, didn't include all of the kids in a population who had surgery, nor were they *randomly selected* from the patient rosters. They were hand picked. Randomization is critical to help ensure that we're not just hearing about the rosiest outcomes, and that the study group reflects the typical patient.

FAST FACT

According to the California Office of Statewide Health Planning and Development database, of those thirteen to twenty years old undergoing bariatric surgery in the state between 2005 and 2007, a disproportionate number were white females.

These eleven young people also represent an infinitesimally tiny percentage—less than 0.4%—of the bariatric surgeries that have been performed on teens. An analysis of national trends in bariatric surgeries for teens was published in the March 2007 issue of *Archives of Pediatric and Adolescent Medicine*. It was conducted by Dr. Inge, along with colleagues at Robert Wood Johnson Medical School at the University of Medicine & Dentistry of New Jersey. They estimated that 2,744 bariatric surgeries had been performed on adolescents in the United States between 1996 and 2003, with 771 in 2003 alone. More than 70 teens had had bariatric surgery just at Cincinnati Children's since 2001, said Dr. Inge in an accompanying press release two years ago [2007].

Yet, only eleven were chosen.

We know nothing about what happened to the thousands of other teens who had bariatric surgery, so no one can possibly conclude that the surgery is a safe medical intervention. How many of those others died or have been left with innumerable complications? How have their physical and psychological health, growth and development been affected? Eleven anecdotal reports, just like testimonials, do not allow us to weigh the risks.

When the control group being used for comparison is also hand picked, it increases risks for stacking the deck.

Girls made up about 60% of both groups in this report, but otherwise, the control group bore little resemblance to the 11 bariatric surgery patients. They were 2½ years younger—average age nearly 15.5 years at the start of the year, compared to 18 years of age in the surgical group. They weighed an average of *105.6 pounds less* (with only 8 kids with BMIs [body mass indexes] in the range of the bariatric group). Fasting blood sugars, insulin levels or HOMA-2 scores (estimates of insulin resistance, although normal values for adolescents have never been published) were not reported for the control group, but they did have *7–26% higher HbA1c* levels (surrogate measures of glucose levels). It is well-known that a normal part of human development is the transient insulin resistance that occurs during puberty, more so in girls and Blacks, which drops down to nearly prepubertal levels by early adulthood. There were no Blacks among the bariatric patient group and race/ethnicity was not reported for the control group. HbA1c levels also vary according to duration of diabetes, being highest during the first two years then dropping. No information was given about the duration of diabetes among either selected group, although the higher levels seen in the younger control group might also have been weighted by duration of their disease.

In other words, no credible comparisons between these very different groups, with key variables uncontrolled, can be made.

Vast Overstatements

This study claimed that in all but one of the teens, their type 2 diabetes had been cured almost before leaving the hospital. This was based on discontinued glycemic medication use during the first 12 months post-op. One explanation why weight loss didn't eliminate the need for medication in that young man was that his diabetes was more advanced than the other adolescents, said Dr. Inge.

The authors admitted that not only did they have limited lab results on the kids, but also that there was no standardization of laboratory assays [analyses] for any of the lab tests reported in this study. At the end of the one-year study period, HbA1c levels were only available for *5 of the 11 teens.* Yet, incredibly, the authors stated that they had "for the first time, to our knowledge, detailed the clinical and metabolic changes that might be expected for adolescents with type 2 diabetes who undergo RYGB [Roux-en-Y gastric bypass]."

No pediatrician would actually consider lab results on five kids to be detailed clinical information or to give an accurate indication of what can be expected for all patients referred for bariatric surgery.

More important, a drop in blood sugar does not mean the underlying disease pathology of diabetes has been cured or reversed. Blood sugars are a symptom, a surrogate endpoint, not *the disease of diabetes* itself. . . . Transient drops in blood glucose levels and other health indices during the short-term clinical trials done to date have reflected the degree of caloric restriction and weight loss, not actual glycemic improvement, or shown to be sustained, as Dr. [Francesco] Rubino and Dr. Jacques Marescaux, M.D., FRCS at the University Louis Pasteur in France explained. Claims that bariatric surgery results in a remission of type 2 diabetes are not supported scientifically, they said, and no study has been designed to specifically test if surgery is an effective treatment and leads to better long-term health outcomes for people with type 2 diabetes, and with benefits that outweigh the risks. As they explained:

> [A] small, uncontrolled case-series type of study is not the proper instrument to demonstrate a direct effect of surgery on type 2 diabetes as there are several possible reasons that could justify improved glycemia after a bariatric operation. For instance, since patients undergoing Roux-en-Y gastric bypass or biliopancreatic diversion

eat small, rather fluid and low-caloric meals in the early postoperative period, it is admittedly impracticable to rule out that the rapid normalization of plasma glucose and improved insulin resistance after these surgeries be simply the effect of decreased caloric intake.

Most disturbing in the claims swirling around this tiny report have been the impressions given that the surgery is safe and will reduce premature deaths from heart disease and other diabetes-related health problems. Besides not reporting any hard clinical outcomes, this study was too short to credibly suggest long-term health benefits—and especially, to investigate risks for long-term complications.

Yet, the authors overstated the conclusions even possible from their case report, writing:

> We also demonstrate that a small group of adolescents with T2DM [type 2 diabetes mellitus] can undergo a major operation safely. These data may prove useful for clinical decision making. . . . The lack of any major medical or surgical complications suggests that the risk/benefit ratio for RYGB in adolescents with T2DM is favorable.

> In addition, the magnitude of the improvement in T2DM disease status, as measured by HbA1c and medication usage, may well be superior with surgery.

> CONCLUSIONS. Our observations provide evidence that bariatric surgery reverses or significantly improves T2DM in adolescents over a 1-year period, further supporting the role of surgery outlined in recent (AAP) [American Academy of Pediatrics] treatment recommendations.

Most readers likely missed the qualifiers *can, may,* and *suggests.* Their later disclaimer—"However, the long-term safety and efficacy of bariatric surgery in adolescents remains to be firmly established."—also had little effect on moderating the sensational news coverage.

Missing Balance

Rather than another paper reporting apparent favorable results seen during the initial honeymoon period of weight loss, why not publish a much more valuable follow-up report on how earlier gastric bypass patients are doing six to ten years later? Or even how *these 11 patients* are doing today? Dr. Inge and colleagues at Cincinnati Children's have previously published articles about serious complications and the desperate need for long-term data on bariatric surgeries on teens.

As covered in more detail here, in their 2007 review of bariatric procedures in teens, they reported "profound" complications seen among procedures done on adolescents through the mid-1990s. The newest and current variations of gastric bypass surgeries, RYGB, has limited evidence in teens, they said. The largest retrospective study in teens with the longest follow-up to date, they wrote, was on 33 adolescents (average age 16) who had RYGB and variations. The surgeons reported that nine teens had major complications within 30 days of surgery, one died one year later and another at six years. All were still obese at every year measured after surgery. More importantly, they noted, all but six were lost in follow-up, with no data available on their status by 14 years.

Three other centers performing laparoscopic gastric bypass on a total of 41 teens since 2005 reported that 39% had complications, two of which had long-term consequences, including a death. While gastric banding "seems to be a technically safer operation with lower mortality risks than other procedures," they said, "systematically collected information about both efficacy and potentially worrisome complications (5–10 years) later . . . for adolescents who have perhaps five or six decades to live with the device" make long-term information about efficacy needed. Despite claims that teens experience fewer post-op complications, recent analyses found they were similar to adults, they said.

Nutritional deficiencies are increased in both restrictive and malabsorption procedures (gastric bypass), they cautioned, and the resulting problems were not insignificant. Peripheral neuropathy is one of the most common vitamin deficiency manifestations, occurring in up to 16% of patients. They described their own 2004 study reporting on three teen girls they were following who experienced neurological complications from thiamine [vitamin B1] deficiency. The girls, 14 to 17 years of age, developed a range of neurological symptoms, including hearing loss, dizziness, numbness and pain in extremities; vomiting; weakness and loss of strength, and inability to walk, just 4 to 6 months after their surgeries.

Dr. Inge and colleagues went on to caution about increased risks for iron deficiency anemia seen after gastric bypass, especially in menstruating young women, despite oral iron supplementation. They expressed concerns about

A young woman talks to a consultant at an obesity clinic after bariatric surgery. The author claims that bariatric surgery has not been proven safe and effective for teens. (© **Life in View/ Photo Researchers, Inc.**)

osteoporosis and osteopenia surfacing among patients a decade out from surgery; although they reported that decreased bone mineral density is evident at 9 months, despite normal parathyroid hormone, calcium and vitamin D levels. "Long term data on these adolescents are not yet available," they cautioned.

But healthcare professionals and the public heard nothing about these concerns or other potentially serious complications being seen among bariatric patients. Instead, we got a case report on *eleven* young people who had surgery *5 to 7 years ago*, giving limited results after only their *first 12 months post-op*. It was reported as being a "breakthrough study" showing dramatic results that offer "an optimistic outlook for their future."

And published in a medical journal.

And not one of those more than 300 media stories headlined with: "New report cautions that bariatric surgeries have not yet been shown to have long-term safety or effectiveness in teens."

That's the difference between medical information and marketing.

CHAPTER 3

Personal Experiences with Childhood Obesity

The Pain of Being the Fat Girl

Rebecca Golden

In the following viewpoint Rebecca Golden describes a childhood in which bullying was a constant occurrence from the time she was five years old until she graduated high school. The taunts and cruelty, directed at her because of her weight, came not only from class-mates, but teachers as well, says Golden. It was so bad that Golden hated her life and wanted to kill herself. However, through it all she never hated herself, never felt like she deserved to be treated so cruelly. Instead she learned defiance and confidence. Golden writes for *Salon* and blogs at *Butterbabe*. She is also the author of the 2009 book *Butterbabe: The True Adventures of a 40-Stone Outsider*.

Photo on previous page. Overweight and obese people suffer discrimination in many areas of life.
(© Christian Darkin/Photo Researchers, Inc.)

At age 5, the last age at which I had a normal body mass, the school football coach's son punched me in the face. I have no memory of what prompted this; small boys can be a strange and violent people. I tasted blood before I felt pain. I am usually quick with a clever line, but the perfect comeback always escaped me in those moments. No matter how many times it happened, I was always surprised, devastated anew by the meanness, by the cutting words, by a classmate's fist.

But soon, they were calling me fat. I wore the ugly Catholic school uniform, a brown plaid pinafore with a white blouse and Peter Pan collar. Under this hot mess, I wore cheap polyester pants, also brown. All the girls had them.

Becoming the Fat Girl

"Fat pig, fat girl, *fat thing!*" This boy never had a name. He was older, in another grade. He threw one of the red rubber balls at me, hitting me in the stomach, laughing as the weight knocked the wind out of me, leaving me gasping for breath on the ground. Catholic school, that failed experiment in my religious education, ended shortly afterward.

Being "the fat girl" happened suddenly. In fact, it happened before I was actually, medically, fat. When children started teasing me, I probably only weighed five pounds more than I should have for my height. But kids seize on small differences. The tall child is a beanstalk, the short kid is a shrimp. By the time my weight became a problem—when I really *was* the fattest person (adults included) in school—I had long since given up weighing myself or caring. Making it through each brutal day became the only goal. The rest of it—my health, my body— fell away. By the time I cared again, after I graduated from high school, I weighed nearly 400 pounds.

At public school in the new-money suburb my parents worked so hard to put us in, the children found a wide array of ways to torture me. I never thought of myself as a child. I never thought of myself as anything, really. I read books, and I learned that girls have best friends. But I had no friends. Kids who liked me when we were alone never acknowledged any relationship with others present. I never really knew who I hated more—the ones who hated me, or the ones who liked me, but only in private.

"Moose, Moose, Moose, Moose, MOOOOSE!" I sat on the hard, cold floor of the school gym, like I did every day, waiting for the bus. Kids chanted, some from my class, some from other grades. Older children, younger children, strangers—they knew my name, the one that Brad, the sixth grader who lived in the house behind mine, had conferred. I heard this chant in line. I heard it on the bus. I heard it on the playground. I heard it every day of my life, every school day, for four years.

In sixth grade, the teacher joined in.

Shocking Cruelty

"Not you!" she shouted, taking the paperback book out of my hands. She'd instructed the class to read silently. I opened a book, relieved at the chance to go someplace else for a while. She threw the book across the room. I remember her angry face, the flecks of foamy spit at the corners of her mouth, how deep wrinkles framed her nose. Her dentures didn't fit properly, and her mouth never closed all the way. She called me "butterball" and pointed out the shiny smear of blood the day I got my period in class. She crowed at the discovery while my classmates shrieked with laughter. When I talk about these things, I marvel at the absurdity and the shocking level of cruelty. It seems like something that would happen to a stranger, something that would happen in a book. All I know is that this was my life. I was 12 years old, and school wasn't safe. I went home and thought about how I would kill myself.

I moved from sixth grade to junior high school in a fog. I felt sad and afraid every day. I never had friends who stood by me. Teachers knew I was smart. They saw the test scores. They read my papers. None of them seemed to wonder why I did so poorly, especially in subjects that required verbal ability. I found it hard to focus because the fear never went away, not even when teachers were around. There was a boy in my art class who talked about his pubic hair and all the girls he'd touched. He leered at me and winked and then laughed with his friends about how easily he could land the whale.

Another boy at our table told me daily how much I disgusted him. He hated me in a quiet, powerful way. One day, our art teacher made us draw pictures of one another, of our hair. My hair tangled easily and I never quite managed to get out all the knots. The quiet boy had talent. He drew my ugly, tangled hair perfectly, paying special attention to the frizzy bump on the back of my head where I tried to hide a particular matted clump.

I longed to be invisible. I worried that anything I did that made me stand out—even good things, like drawing well or writing a story for the school paper—would mean attracting the wrong kind of attention. I loved to draw and paint, but I stopped taking art class in ninth grade because after our teacher left to smoke, a junior in the class went up to the board and drew pictures of me, nude and in impossible sexual positions.

One boy stabbed me with a pen. He pinned me against the wall in basic algebra—a class for math dummies—and told his friends to watch.

"I bet she bleeds gravy," he said, jabbing my bare arm. I bled. I cried. I trembled. I know I should've screamed, or done something else to attract the attention of the wrestling coach in charge of the class, sitting at his desk and prying bits of black scum out from under his fingernails with a pocketknife, but I couldn't actually believe this was happening until it was over. Even then, I couldn't make a sound. I didn't move until long after the bell rang and the classroom had emptied completely.

FAST FACT

According to the report *F as in Fat 2011,* issued by Trust for America's Health and the Robert Woods Johnson Foundation, data from 2007 reveal that Mississippi had the highest rate (21.9 percent) and Oregon had the lowest rate (9.6 percent) of obesity among those aged ten to seventeen years.

Defiance Was All I Had

We've heard so much about the tragic consequences of bullying lately. Facebook and other social networks have added a new, baffling dimension to children's attacks on each other. But long before "bullying" was a national conversation, there were people like me. People who faced a gantlet of assault, taunting, humiliation and sexual harassment, people who were denied meaningful parts of their education. The children—who, famously, can be so cruel—were as advertised. And in my life, the adults either didn't care, couldn't be bothered, didn't notice or actively participated. My advanced-placement European history teacher, a self-proclaimed feminist who wore a pro-choice coat hanger on a necklace but never called on girls in class, called me stupid in front of the students. When I asked her for help preparing for a test, she told me to get out of her sight. I think looking at me actually made her sick.

People who tried to help thought the best way to end this daily nightmare would be for me to do the right thing and lose weight. My parents called the school, complained to individual teachers and gave me bad advice. "Just ignore it," they told me, echoing the ages-old bullying strategy that never works for anyone. "If you ignore them, they'll stop." I have no idea what they should've done, or if anything would've helped. At the time, lectures on my weight just made me angrier and sadder. Given how intensely miserable I was, tending my health was beyond my reach. Suggestions like that infuriated me. Despite my classmates' best efforts, despite my teachers' utter failure to look out for me, despite the callousness of principals and the great distress I caused my own family, I had this crazy idea that I had a right to courtesy and an education no matter what I weighed. This idea made me defiant—and defiance was the only thing I had going for me for a long, long time.

Having Comebacks

I'm still fat. I peaked at about 600 pounds before losing more than half my body weight. Still, I'm not thin, and probably never will be. One day at the gym, after swimming a mile and showering, I heard the sound of teen girls laughing. I saw them behind me, pointing at me as I changed clothes, making whispered comments to one another.

"If you think this is bad, you should've seen me before I lost 300 pounds," I told them. I stared them down. There were shamefaced and murmured apologies. At 35, I finally managed to win a round with some mean girls. Hooray for me, I thought.

But despite it all, I think people may be good. The recent public outrage over bullying gay teens makes me believe that. Efforts by [advice columnist] Dan Savage and others inspire me to hold on to this thought. I have no regrets about not killing myself at 12. I've been to Australia, loved good people, had amazing friends and even written a book. I manage to have comebacks all the time now.

"Hey, baby," a 14-year-old boy at the mall thinks he'll make a scene and entertain his friends.

"Call me when you grow some pubes," I tell him. His friends laugh. He scowls and tells them to shut up. I triumph over a bully. Over a child, really. I know it's petty, and that I have other reasons to feel good about myself and to let go of the ugliness of my school days. I know that. But I'll take what I can get.

Parents Should Not Be Blamed for Their Children's Obesity

Stacey R. Hall

In the following viewpoint Stacey R. Hall decries the notion that parents should be labeled as abusive if their children are obese. Hall explains that she has been fat since she was a toddler. She does not take personally all the derision and hate that she says society levels against fat people. She cannot accept, however, that anyone would criticize her parents for her weight problem. They may not have always done the right thing when it came to food, but they tried, she says. They overcame adversity to give her and her siblings a comfortable life full of opportunity, happiness, and health, insists Hall. Hall is a writer based in southwestern Ohio.

I was channel surfing mindlessly, avoiding some household chore, when I landed on a cable talk show discussing child abuse. The guests were talking about horrible things: parents who starve children, beat them or sexually abuse them. Parents who let their children get fat. This last one, one woman leveled, was the same as any other form of abuse and deserved the same unequivocal response: Remove the kids from the parents.

I had happened upon yet another media debate in response to the controversial *JAMA* [*Journal of the American Medical Association*] article that came out a few weeks ago [July 2011]. This study looked at whether intervention was ever warranted when parents allow their children to become dangerously obese. The study itself was balanced in its approach, but the talking-head response was anything but. This particular pundit—shoulder-shrugging with a clear look of disgust on her face—talked about taking fat kids away from their parents as if it were nothing more than trading in a car. I had to turn the TV off, my stomach in knots.

I wondered what this woman would say if she met my own parents. Would she blame them for the way I turned out? For that matter: Should I?

I Can Handle the Stigma of Being Fat

Let me back up a bit. I'm fat and have been since I was a toddler. Not "trapped in my trailer" fat, or "have to use an extra-wide electric wheelchair at the grocery store" fat, but medically, technically, morbidly obese. I confess that whenever I hear that term—morbidly obese—I giggle, because I picture chubby Goths with black nail polish and dog collars. That is not to say I do not take it seriously, because I do. It is the first thing I think about when I wake up in the morning, the last thing on my mind when I go to bed at night. And I will never be a member of the "fat acceptance movement," because I don't accept it. I have been fighting my weight for over 35 years.

But I don't believe I deserve to be hated, and hate is what I feel every single day as a fat woman. I feel it in the stares from strangers' children, and when someone screams "fat ass" as I walk my dogs. I feel it when I get a flawless performance review, but my boss asks if I have considered weight loss surgery—as if that has something to do with my professional skills. I feel it in the constant stream of media images about what women should look like, in the tired fat jokes from comedians (come on, stop phoning it in—get creative!), and in the constant articles about the doom that is The Obesity Epidemic. Fat people are taxing the healthcare system, they make other people uncomfortable on planes and trains, they use more fossil fuels because it takes more gas to haul their big butts around thus causing global warming, and they suck up the world's food resources while others starve.

And yet, I understand: These arguments aren't without merit, and it is after all human nature that some people express their points with meanness and derision. I don't take it personally.

Do Not Blame My Parents

But even at my most open-minded, I could not bear the debate that erupted in response to the *JAMA* article (and the derisive online comments). While the study, by Dr. David Ludwig and Lindsey Murtagh, did suggest that obese children—in some extreme circumstances—should be taken away from their parents, coverage of the article focused on the most sensational elements of the argument. It resulted in a cascade of hate on cable news and morning shows that was packaged as concern for children, like that disgusted-looking pundit who made me sick to my stomach.

Did my parents make me fat? Probably. They fed my siblings and me meals of bologna on white bread, hot dogs and potato chips. They let us have four of those Oreo-knock-off cookies-that-don't-quite-taste-right in a sitting, rather than one or two. They used fast food as a reward and eating in general as a form of entertainment. If I was upset, I might be offered a tasty snack as a pick-me-up. Even if nothing got done all day, not the dishes, not the vacuuming, not mowing the lawn, by god dinner would get done and there wouldn't be any leftovers to pack up and put away. I suppose to some people it is a portrait of failed parenting.

But my parents are also a success story. They were teen parents. They had me—the eldest—at age 16. It was not a mistake but a planned pregnancy. My mother grew up in a household where she faced daily abuse at the hands of people she trusted. There were challenging finances and in a family with eight children, food could sometimes be scarce. My father grew up in a slightly more stable financial situation, but where violence was the primary outlet for anger, or disappointment, as well as for discipline of children. When these two wounded, but hopeful souls met they made a forever pact in heart-shaped doodles on their class notebooks. They crafted an escape plan: Create their own family where they would make different rules. That is just what they did.

And they did it all on their own. My dad worked two jobs while finishing high school. My mom went back to night school after I was born. Dad worked double night shifts and Mom cut coupons and raised the kids while balancing work at McDonald's. They never got welfare. They never received food stamps. They modeled hard work and commitment and most of all, love. They are still married—still go out on date nights and still laugh and look longingly in each other's eyes—almost 40 years later.

Doctors did warn them about the children's weight, and these problems were not ignored. My mom worried. She ached for me when I came home crying after schoolmates teased me all day long. She was my biggest cheerleader when, in the fifth grade, I became the youngest member of the local Weight Watchers group to reach the 50-pound weight loss mark. She saved money we didn't have to buy weight-loss shakes and exercise equipment.

> **FAST FACT**
>
> Childhood obesity is the number one health concern among parents in the United States, topping drug abuse and smoking, according to the C.S. Mott Children's Hospital National Poll on Children's Health, 2010.

She went without sleep sewing cute clothes that actually fit well, unlike the pricey crap in the husky department. Dad did his best when he wasn't working.

But once the fat is on, it is hard to get it off. When you get it off, it comes back with a vengeance. My parents could never quite bridge the gap between what was recommended and what we could afford, between what they went without and what they would never allow us to miss. And who's to say what part their parenting played in all this, really—which part was simple genetics and which part was the learned behavior of emotional eating; which part overindulgence and which part the negative side effects of yo-yo dieting; which part was uncooperative children and which part plain lack of knowledge and time. To think of that pundit giving such a disgusted look to my parents, crushes me. They tried so hard. They, in fact, did way more than so many. From troubled beginnings, they created a family where the cycle of violence was broken, where their children had access to more education and opportunity than they had. Did they make mistakes with food? Yes. But there was nobody better to raise my siblings and me than the two people who sacrificed so much to make sure we grew up happier and healthier than they had.

That's the real point here: We are healthier for their efforts. No matter our size.

Changing Perceptions of Obesity—Recollections of a Paediatrician

Louise A. Baur

In the following viewpoint pediatrician Louise A. Baur considers how childhood obesity has grown from a disorder that pediatricians seldom encountered to one that pediatricians commonly see on a daily basis. Baur says that when she first decided to establish a clinic to see children with obesity-related disorders, many of her colleagues reacted with strong negative emotions. Over the years, Baur says she has learned how to change the perceptions of her colleagues and educate other doctors about childhood obesity. Baur is an Australian pediatrician and a professor at the University of Sydney Medical School and School of Public Health.

It's a Monday morning. I'm in my clinic and the consultation with my first patient is just ending. We've discussed management of his obesity (body-mass index [BMI] 34 kg/m^2) and prediabetes, and review the healthy lifestyle changes that have been made. There's been an encouraging reduction in weight and waist circumference since I last saw him. I emphasise the importance of ongoing support from the dietitian and clinical psychologist, adjust metformin dosage, and discuss follow up arrangements. The next patient is new to the clinic and is more severely obese (BMI 44 kg/m^2). She is referred from a sleep physician and has recently started continuous positive airway pressure therapy for her obstructive sleep apnoea. That treatment at least is going well—she recounts being more refreshed in the morning and less sleepy during the day. I review the blood test results and realise that she has prediabetes, dyslipidaemia and probable fatty liver disease. Further history shows she has a number of psychological problems associated with her obesity and probable depression. Clinical examination reveals high blood pressure as well as thickened, pigmented skin at the base of her neck and in the flexures. I recognise acanthosis nigricans, characteristic of insulin resistance. Management will be a challenge. What treatment options should I broach?

These are typical stories of the many patients with obesity-related chronic disease seen by medical practitioners. But what if I tell you that the clinic is in a children's hospital, with both patients aged only 11 years, and neither yet at high school? We should rightly be shocked by such a situation. We do not expect children to be on medication for treatment of prediabetes. Nor do we consider it normal for them to be on a machine in order to sleep at night without stopping breathing. If there were a doubt about the impact of obesity on the health and wellbeing of young people, then the experience of clinicians at my hospital, and in many such facilities around the world, dispels it readily. Each week sleep physicians are diagnosing obstructive sleep apnoea in obese children more frequently, orthopaedic surgeons are pinning more slipped upper femoral epiphyses, and endocrinologists are managing increasing numbers of young people with type 2 diabetes and prediabetes. Severe obesity is certainly contributing to increased health-care costs in paediatric institutions.

Paediatric obesity, as a recognised and common health problem, seems to have come upon the health system fairly quickly. I recall that during my 5 years as a medical student in the late 1970s, I received one 60 minute lecture on adult obesity. In my subsequent training to be a paediatrician during the 1980s, the issue of obesity was barely discussed, and then only in the context of rare genetic disorders, such as Prader-Willi syndrome. Type 2 diabetes, which is linked to obesity, was known as "adult-onset diabetes" because it was never seen in a paediatric setting. Now, in the 21st century, type 2 diabetes is seen in teenagers and even younger children, and obesity is a national health priority in Australia and many other countries. Although there has been a recent plateauing of childhood obesity in several countries in western Europe, and in Australia, Japan, and the USA, prevalence rates remain unacceptably high, and they continue to rise in eastern Europe and many countries undergoing nutrition transition. And those children who are obese seem to be more severely obese and to have a greater central fat distribution.

Another recollection: it's 1991 and I am planning my postdoctoral studies in an endocrinology unit at an adult hospital. I want to learn about obesity since I suspect it may be useful knowledge for a paediatrician interested in nutritional problems. My future supervisor, a nutritional biochemist, talks enthusiastically about the research work we will do, emphasising the importance of understanding the muscle metabolic abnormalities underlying syndrome X, or the metabolic syndrome. I suddenly feel embarrassed—have no idea what he is talking about. Metabolic syndrome? Syndrome X? What does he mean? I listen intently to his explanation and then hurry to the medical library for more information. But I find only a few papers in the research literature on that subject, and certainly nothing relevant to children. But now, in 2011, a quick search on the internet shows 4.83 million entries on the subject of the metabolic syndrome. 20 years on, this topic has become the stuff of internet traffic and everyday discourse.

And now a further series of memories, beginning in the mid-1990s when I am a consultant paediatrician. I am excited about the possibilities of establishing a clinical service for obese and insulin-resistant children and young people. I am sure that others must also see the great unmet clinical need. Indeed, several colleagues are very supportive of the idea—they, too, are seeing patients with obesity-associated comorbidities and are struggling with management. However, I also encounter a range of markedly different attitudes from others—disinterest, antipathy, and even outright resistance. One colleague has dubbed these phenomena the "obesity resistance syndrome (ORS)".

Why should obesity arouse strong negative emotions in some clinicians? Perhaps there is an unthinking acceptance of some of the prevailing community misperceptions of obesity? Some seem to view obesity as the result of moral failure—of gluttony and sloth, and a lack of personal responsibility. A few have a sense of therapeutic nihilism about obesity: no treatment works, so why bother? Still others are anxious about managing people with obesity since they have had little, if any, training in the area. Such views are often unstated, but can be deeply embedded. My experience of establishing a clinical service for obese children and young people with this as a background provides strikingly vivid images and memories. I have learnt several lessons in the process.

One important lesson was to talk to other clinicians about my patients in ways that might be heard and which addressed misperceptions. Take this example, told to a referring doctor, in the presence of a group of fellow paediatricians: "We had a great clinic this morning. You remember YY, the 15-year-old Turkish boy with prediabetes and severe obesity, whose parents both have type 2 diabetes? Well, he's been seeing the dietitian regularly and it's really helped—he's lost 14 kg in the past 4 months, he's no longer on the metformin, and he seems to have really taken the lifestyle changes on board for himself." The not-so-subtle subtexts of this story are that treatment can lead to successful outcomes, and frequent therapist support may be vital. Or this comment, spoken to a neurologist who expressed the view that successful obesity treatment should be possible with only one or two clinic visits. "But isn't your patient with epilepsy whom you've been seeing for 4 years, still needing anti-epileptic therapy? Perhaps there are parallels with obesity?" This sort of remark, which I learnt to modify to suit the relevant specialty, says that obesity is a chronic, potentially life-long, condition and obesity management should be approached in a similar way to that of other chronic diseases.

Another strategy was to tell the stories of selected patients so that clinicians and administrators could hear about the impact of obesity on their lives. On one memorable occasion, a paediatrician interviewed an adolescent boy with very severe obesity, about his illness, in front of a lecture theatre full of doctors attending a paediatric training day. It was beautifully done, with great sensitivity. The room was hushed as the audience listened to this young man talk about what the disease had cost him and his family, both socially and emotionally. That session was the most highly evaluated part of the day. Several people said that their whole view of obesity had changed, simply by hearing this boy's story.

A further important lesson was to focus part of the work of the weight management staff on the training

FAST FACT

Among US children aged two to four years, American Indian and Alaska Native (20.7 percent) and Hispanic (17.9 percent) have the highest rates of obesity, according to data from the 2009 Pediatric Nutrition Surveillance System.

needs of other clinicians, and not just on clinical service delivery to patients affected by obesity. Because obesity is a fairly new paediatric disorder, we realised there were no established clinical training services, as you might expect for other prevalent health problems of childhood. However, many clinicians were hungry for information. My colleagues and I found ourselves busy providing ongoing education sessions at undergraduate and postgraduate level, to a range of health professionals, and in many settings. We have become more strategic in recent years, focusing on larger group teaching, targeting specific groups, and developing online training modules.

The final lesson was to work towards making obesity the concern of many people within the hospital organisation, and not to have it seen solely as the responsibility of a few enthusiastic clinicians. While the latter approach might conceivably work for a rare disorder, it is simply not viable for such a common problem as obesity. Several strategies helped. My colleagues and I presented on the issue of obesity at various meetings, both within the hospital and beyond. We did surveys that showed how large numbers of obese patients were attending healthcare settings for a variety of reasons, but usually were not being treated for the problem of obesity. And we repeatedly emphasised the broader national concerns about childhood obesity that were developing over this period.

These various lessons now form part of the many memories of obesity that I have acquired. From a topic that received a modicum of teaching time when I was a medical student, it has now become a part of routine clinical experience for many health professionals, including myself, and a focus of population health campaigns in many countries. What will the next few decades see in terms of the evolution of obesity? I muse on this question as I start to read my next patient's notes: she is 7 years old with a weight of almost 55 kg. No time to reminisce—there's work to be done.

GLOSSARY

absolute intensity   The amount of energy used by the body per minute of activity.

aerobic exercise   Physical activity using the same large muscle group, rhythmically, for a period of fifteen to twenty minutes or longer while maintaining 60–80 percent of maximum heart rate. Aerobic exercise conditions the heart and lungs by increasing the oxygen available to the body and by enabling the heart to use oxygen more efficiently.

atherosclerosis   A process whereby fat, cholesterol, and other substances build up in the walls of arteries and form hard structures called plaques. Also called hardening of the arteries, atherosclerosis makes it harder for blood to flow through the arteries.

bariatric surgery   Surgery on the stomach and/or intestines to help patients with extreme obesity to lose weight.

body mass index (BMI)   A measure used to determine overweight and obesity. It is calculated using weight and height. BMI does not measure body fat directly, but it is a reasonable indicator of body fatness.

calorie   The unit of measure for the amount of energy stored in food. One calorie is the amount of energy required to raise the temperature of one gram of water one degree centigrade.

carbohydrate   A biological molecule consisting only of carbon, hydrogen, and oxygen, which is a major source of energy in many foods. There are two kinds of carbohydrates: simple carbohydrates and complex carbohydrates. Simple carbohydrates are sugars, like sucrose and glucose. Complex carbohydrates include starches and fiber.

cardiovascular disease (CVD)   Diseases of the heart and blood vessels, many of which are related to atherosclerosis.

cholesterol	A fat-like substance that is made by the body and is found naturally in animal foods such as meat, fish, poultry, eggs, and dairy products. Cholesterol is transported in the blood in low-density lipoproteins and high-density lipoproteins.
chronic disease	A disease of long duration and generally slow progression, such as heart disease, stroke, and diabetes.
cognitive-behavioral therapy (CBT)	A psychotherapeutic approach that emphasizes correcting distorted thinking patterns and changing one's behaviors accordingly.
Daily Reference Value (DRV)	One of the two sets of reference values established by the US Food and Drug Administration (FDA) for reporting nutrients in nutrition labeling. The DRVs assist consumers in interpreting information about the amount of a nutrient that is present in a food and in comparing nutritional values of food products. DRVs are established for adults and children four or more years of age and provide information about total fat, saturated fat, cholesterol, total carbohydrate, dietary fiber, sodium, potassium, and protein.
diabetes	A chronic disease in which there are high levels of glucose in the blood. Diabetes occurs when the pancreas does not make enough insulin, the hormone that controls blood glucose levels, or the body does not respond to the insulin that is made. There are two main types of diabetes: type 1 and type 2.
Dietary Guidelines for Americans (DGA)	Guidelines issued by the US Department of Health and Human Services and the US Department of Agriculture (USDA) that provide advice for making food choices that help promote good health, maintain a healthy weight, and prevent disease.
Dietary Reference Intake (DRI)	A system of nutrition recommendations issued by the Institute of Medicine and used by the United States and Canada. DRIs succeeded the Recommended Dietary Allowance (RDA). DRIs are used to determine the composition of diets for schools, prisons, hospitals, and nursing homes; by industries to develop new foodstuffs; and by health care policy makers and public health officials. The DRI values are not currently used in nutrition labeling.

energy balance   The balance of calories consumed through eating and drinking compared to calories burned through physical activity.

fat   Biological molecules that are made up of carbon, hydrogen, and oxygen. They are a source of energy in foods. Fats belong to a group of substances called lipids and come in liquid or solid form. All fats are combinations of saturated and unsaturated fatty acids.

genetic predisposition   An increased susceptibility to a particular disease due to the presence of one or more gene mutations.

glucose   Sugar, a building block for most carbohydrates. After digestion, glucose is carried in the blood and goes to body cells, where it is used for energy or stored.

healthy weight   Compared to overweight or obese, a body weight that is less likely to be linked with any weight-related health problems. A BMI of 18.5 to 24.9 is considered a healthy weight.

high-density lipoprotein (HDL)   A biological molecule made up of proteins and fats that carries cholesterol to the liver. Commonly known as "good cholesterol," high levels of HDL lower the risk of heart disease.

hydrogenation   A chemical process that turns liquid fat (oil) into solid fat. This process creates a new fat called trans fat, which is associated with heart disease.

hypothyroidism   Deficient thyroid gland activity, resulting in a lowered metabolic rate.

insulin   A hormone made by the pancreas that helps move glucose (sugar) from the blood to muscles and other tissues. Insulin controls blood sugar levels.

lifestyle factors   Behavior habits that can negatively affect health, such as smoking or watching TV, or that can positively affect health, such as daily exercise and healthy eating habits.

lipoprotein   Biological substances made up of fat and protein that carry fats and fat-like substances, such as cholesterol, in the blood.

low-density lipoprotein (LDL)	A biological molecule made up of proteins and fats that carry cholesterol in the body. Commonly called "bad" cholesterol, high levels of LDL increase the risk of heart disease.
metabolism	The set of chemical reactions that happen in the cells of living organisms to sustain life. Metabolism is usually divided into two categories. Catabolism breaks down food to harvest energy, while anabolism uses energy to construct components of cells such as proteins and carbohydrates.
moderate-intensity physical activity	On an absolute scale, physical activity that is done at 3.0 to 5.9 times the intensity of rest.
obesity (child)	Defined as a BMI at or above the 95th percentile for children of the same age and sex.
overweight (child)	Defined as a BMI at or above the 85th percentile and lower than the 95th percentile for children of the same age and sex.
percent daily value (%DV)	A term on food labels based on either the DRI or the Reference Daily Intake (RDI), which provides information on the percent of the daily recommended amount of the nutrient that a serving of the food provides. The %DVs are based on a daily intake of two thousand calories. The %DV also provides a basis for thresholds that define descriptive words for nutrient content, such as "high fiber" or "low fat."
physical activity	Any form of exercise or movement.
physical fitness	The ability to carry out daily tasks with vigor and alertness, without undue fatigue, and with ample energy to enjoy leisure-time pursuits and respond to emergencies.
Prader-Willi syndrome	An uncommon genetic disorder that causes a constant feeling of hunger.
protein	An essential nutrient composed of amino acids that helps build many parts of the body, including muscle, bone, skin, and blood. Proteins are found in foods like meat, fish, poultry, eggs, dairy products, beans, nuts, and tofu.

Recommended Dietary Allowance (RDA)	An older set of dietary recommendations made by the USDA. In 1997 the RDA became one part of a broader set of dietary guidelines called the Dietary Reference Intake, used by both the United States and Canada.
Reference Daily Intake (RDI)	One of the two sets of reference values established by the FDA for reporting nutrients on food labels. RDIs assist consumers in interpreting information about the amount of a nutrient that is present in a food and in comparing nutritional values of food products. RDIs are provided for vitamins and minerals, and for protein for children less than four years of age and for pregnant and lactating women.
saturated fat	A fat that is solid at room temperature. Saturated fat is found in high-fat dairy products (like cheese, whole milk, cream, butter, and regular ice cream), ready-to-eat meats, the skin and fat of chicken and turkey, lard, palm oil, and coconut oil. Saturated fats are linked to coronary heart disease.
trans fat	A fat that is produced when liquid fat (oil) is turned into solid fat through a chemical process called hydrogenation. Trans fats have been linked to heart disease.
type 1 diabetes	A type of diabetes that is most often diagnosed in children, teens, or young adults. In this disease, the body makes little or no insulin. Daily injections of insulin are needed.
type 2 diabetes	The most common form of diabetes, it most often occurs in adulthood but is becoming increasingly common in teens and young adults.
vigorous-intensity physical activity	On an absolute scale, physical activity that is done at six or more times the intensity of rest.

CHRONOLOGY

B.C. ca. 8000 to 7000 Sugarcane appears on the island of New Guinea and gradually spreads across the world.

A.D. 1825 Frenchman Jean Anthelme Brillat-Savarin discusses the causes of obesity in his book *The Physiology of Taste.* According to Brillat-Savarin, "Obesity is that state of greasy congestion in which without the sufferer being sick, the limbs gradually increase in volume, and lose their form and harmony."

1863 Englishman William Banting publishes *Letter on Corpulence, Addressed to the Public.* The pamphlet, which details how Banting lost sixty-five pounds by limiting carbohydrates, is considered the first "diet book."

1886 John Pemberton, an Atlanta pharmacist, begins selling Coca-Cola for five cents a glass.

1911 Procter & Gamble introduces Crisco hydrogenated cottonseed oil.

1941 The Recommended Dietary Allowance (RDA) is developed by Lydia J. Roberts, Hazel Stiebeling, and Helen S. Mitchell, all part of a committee established by the National Academy of Sciences to investigate issues of nutrition that might affect national defense.

1946 The National School Lunch Program is established under the National School Lunch Act to provide free or low-cost nutritious school meals to children in order to help promote their health and well-being.

1953   Hans Kraus, an associate professor of physical medicine and rehabilitation at New York University, publishes "Muscular Fitness and Health" in the *Journal of the American Association for Health, Physical Education, and Recreation*, claiming that the nation is becoming soft.

1956   President Dwight D. Eisenhower establishes the President's Council on Youth Fitness.

1966   The Presidential Physical Fitness Award for exceptional achievement is established.

1971–1974   The obesity rate of American children age two to nineteen years is 5 percent.

1979   McDonald's restaurants roll out the Happy Meal, aimed at children, in the United States.

1980   The US Department of Health and Human Services and the US Department of Agriculture USDA publish the first set of Dietary Guidelines for Americans.

1990   The Nutrition Labeling and Education Act is enacted. The law gives the US Food and Drug Administration (FDA) authority to require nutrition labeling of most foods and to require that all nutrient content and health claims meet FDA regulations.

1997   The Dietary Reference Intake is introduced in the United States and Canada.

2000   Children with body mass index (BMI) values at or above the 95th percentile of the sex-specific BMI growth charts are categorized as obese.

2000   The federal government sets a goal of reducing childhood obesity from 13.9 percent to 5 percent by 2010.

2001   The US surgeon general issues the *Call to Action to Prevent and Decrease Overweight and Obesity.*

2002   Arkansas becomes the first state to require BMI percentiles as part of student health records.

2006   The beverage industry announces that it will begin to voluntarily remove high-calorie soft drinks from all US schools.

2007–2008   The obesity rate of American children age two to nineteen years is 16.9 percent.

2010   The Healthy, Hunger-Free Kids Act directs the USDA to set new nutrition standards for all food served in schools.

2010   First Lady Michelle Obama launches Let's Move!, a nationwide campaign to tackle childhood obesity.

ORGANIZATIONS TO CONTACT

The editors have compiled the following list of organizations concerned with the issues debated in this book. The descriptions are derived from materials provided by the organizations. All have publications or information available for interested readers. The list was compiled on the date of publication of the present volume; the information provided here may change. Be aware that many organizations take several weeks or longer to respond to inquiries, so allow as much time as possible.

American Academy of Pediatrics (AAP)
141 Northwest Point Blvd., Elk Grove Village, IL 60007-1098
(847) 434-4000
fax: (847) 434-8000
website: www.aap.org

The AAP is an organization of pediatricians committed to the optimal physical, mental, and social health and well-being for all infants, children, adolescents, and young adults. The AAP offers continuing medical education programs for pediatricians and issues policy statements, clinical reports, clinical practice guidelines, and technical reports. *AAP News* is the official news-magazine of the AAP, while *Pediatrics* is the official journal of the AAP.

American Dietetic Association (ADA)
120 S. Riverside Plaza, Ste. 2000, Chicago, IL 60606
(800) 877-1600
e-mail: hotline@eat right.org
website: webdietitions .org

The ADA is an organization of food and nutrition professionals who are committed to improving the nation's health and advancing the profession of dietetics through research, education, and advocacy. The ADA accomplishes its mission by providing reliable and evidence-based nutrition information for the public, acting as the accrediting agency for graduate and under-graduate nutrition education curricula, credentialing dietetics professionals, and advocating for public policy issues affecting consumers and the practice of dietetics. The ADA publishes a monthly peer-reviewed periodical, the *Journal of the American Dietetic Association*.

Association for Size Diversity and Health (ASDAH)
PO Box 3093, Redwood City, CA 94064
(877) 576-1102
e-mail: www.size diversityandhealth .org/contact.asp
website: www.size diversityandhealth.org

The ASDAH is an international professional organization composed of individual members who are committed to the Health At Every Size® principles. ASDAH's mission is to promote education, research, and the provision of services that enhance health and well-being and are free from weight-based assumptions and weight discrimination. The ASDAH launched a blog in 2011 in which contributors share their experiences with the Health At Every Size approach.

CDC Division of Nutrition, Physical Activity, and Obesity (DNPAO)
1600 Clifton Rd., Atlanta, GA 30333
(800) 232-4636
e-mail: cdcinfo@cdc .gov
website: www.cdc.gov /nccdphp/dnpao/index .html

The DNPAO is part of the Centers for Disease Control and Prevention (CDC), an agency of the US Department of Health and Human Services. The DNPAO works to prevent and control obesity, chronic disease, and other health conditions through regular physical activity and good nutrition. The division supports state health departments, provides funding to reduce obesity and obesity-related diseases, and supports research to enhance the effectiveness of physical activity and nutrition programs. The DNPAO website offers myriad publications on obesity, as well as data such as state obesity rates and physical activity rates.

Center for Science in the Public Interest (CSPI)
1220 L St. NW, Ste. 300, Washington, DC 20005
(202) 332-9110
fax: (202) 265-4954
e-mail: cspi@cspinet .org
website: http://cspinet .org

The mission of the CSPI is to educate the public and advocate for government policies that are consistent with scientific evidence on nutrition, food safety, health, environmental protection, and other issues. The CSPI's goals include eliminating junk food in schools, eliminating partially hydrogenated oil in the American diet, improving food safety laws, and advocating for more healthy, plant-based, environmentally friendly diets, among many other things. The CSPI publishes a monthly newsletter, the *Nutrition Action Healthletter*.

Eunice Kennedy Shriver National Institute of Child Health & Human Development (NICHD)
Bldg. 31, Rm. 2A32, MSC 2425, 31 Center Dr., Bethesda, MD 20892-2425
(800) 370-2943
fax: (866) 760-5947
e-mail: NICHD Information ResourceCenter@mail.nih.gov
website: www.nichd.nih.gov

The NICHD is one of the twenty-seven institutes and centers that make up the National Institutes of Health. The NICHD conducts and supports research on topics related to the health of children, adults, families, and populations. The institute has established a wide-reaching initiative to generate long-term solutions to childhood obesity. The NICHD website provides child health statistics, backgrounders, and many other resources.

Healthy Weight Commitment Foundation
1025 Thomas Jefferson St. NW, Ste. 420 E., Washington, DC 20007
(202) 558-4660
e-mail: info@healthy weightcommit.org
website: www.healthy weightcommit.org

The Healthy Weight Commitment Foundation is a national, multiyear effort designed to help reduce obesity—especially childhood obesity—by 2015. The coalition brings together hundreds of retailers, food and beverage manufacturers, restaurants, sporting goods and insurance companies, trade associations and nongovernmental organizations (NGOs), and professional sports organizations. The foundation promotes ways to help people achieve a healthy weight through energy balance. The foundation spearheads initiatives such as the national Together Counts campaign to encourage families to eat meals together. The foundation also provides many resources for students, teachers, families, and communities, such as Energy Balance 101, a free wellness resource.

International Obesity Task Force (IOTF)
Charles Darwin House, 12 Roger St., London WCIN 2JU, UK
+44 20 7685 2580
fax: +44 20 7685 2581
e-mail: enquiries@iaso
.org
website: www.iaso.org
/iotf

The IOTF is a research-based think tank of international obesity experts and represents the advocacy arm of the International Association for the Study of Obesity. The IOTF's mission is to facilitate a decline in the global obesity burden and narrow its related inequalities in children and adults through effective and sustainable policy and environmental changes. The IOTF catalyzes evidence-informed policy actions for the effective prevention of obesity at national, regional, and global levels.

Obesity Action Coalition (OAC)
4511 N. Himes Ave., Ste. 250, Tampa, FL 33614
(813) 872-7835
fax: (813) 873-7838
e-mail: info@obesity
action.org
website: www.obesity
action.org

The OAC is a national nonprofit organization dedicated to giving a voice to those affected by obesity. The OAC seeks to increase obesity education by offering a wide variety of free educational resources on obesity, morbid obesity, and childhood obesity, in addition to consequences and treatments of these conditions. The OAC also conducts a variety of advocacy efforts throughout the United States on both the national and state levels and encourages individuals to become proactive advocates. The OAC sponsors the Annual Walk from Obesity, which takes place in more than seventy cities across the country in the months of September and October. The OAC's *Your Weight Matters Magazine* is geared toward those affected by obesity and contains a wide variety of educational and advocacy information.

Partnership for a Healthier America (PHA)
(202) 842-9001
e-mail: info@ahealthier
america.org
website: www.ahealth
ieramerica.org

The PHA is a nonpartisan, nonprofit organization devoted to working with the private sector to ensure the health of our nation's youth by solving the childhood obesity crisis. The PHA brings together public, private, and nonprofit leaders to broker meaningful commitments and develop strategies to end childhood obesity. The PHA was founded in conjunction with (but is independent from) the Let's Move! campaign. The PHA sponsors an annual summit and provides facts about childhood obesity and links to resources provided by Let's Move!

Robert Wood John-son Foundation (RWJF)
PO Box 2316, Rte. 1 and College Rd. E., Princeton, NJ 08543
(877) 843-7953
e-mail: www.rwjf.org /global/contactus.jsp
website: www.rwjf.org

The mission of the RWJF is to improve the health and health care of all Americans. The foundation's Childhood Obesity Program seeks to help all children and families eat well and move more—especially those in communities at highest risk for obesity. The foundation's goal is to reverse the childhood obesity epidemic by 2015 by improving access to affordable healthy foods and increasing opportunities for physical activity in schools and communities across the nation. The RWJF website provides charts and maps detailing obesity in the United States, as well as issue and policy briefs on childhood obesity and obesity in general.

Rudd Center for Food Policy & Obesity
Yale University, PO Box 208369, New Haven, CT 06520-8369
(203) 432-6700
fax: (203) 432-9674
e-mail: rudd.center@ yale.edu
website: www.yalerudd center.org

The Rudd Center for Food Policy & Obesity at Yale University is a nonprofit research and public policy organization devoted to improving the world's diet, preventing obesity, and reducing weight stigma. The center serves as a research institution and clearinghouse for resources that add to our understanding of the complex forces affecting how we eat, how we stigmatize overweight and obese people, and how we can change. The study of food marketing to youth is one of the Rudd Center's core research initiatives. The Rudd Center's monthly newsletter, *Health Digest*, is dedicated to spotlighting all of the latest developments in the areas of food policy and obesity.

FOR FURTHER READING

Books

Debasis Bagchi, ed., *Global Perspectives on Childhood Obesity: Current Status, Consequences and Prevention.* Waltham, MA: Academic, 2010.

Francis Berg, *Underage and Overweight: America's Childhood Obesity Epidemic—What Every Parent Needs to Know.* New York: Hatherleigh, 2003.

Kelly Brownell and Katherine Battle Horgen, *Food Fight: The Inside Story of the Food Industry, America's Obesity Crisis, and What We Can Do About It.* New York: McGraw-Hill, 2004.

N. Cameron, N.G. Norgan, and G.T.H. Ellison, eds., *Childhood Obesity: Contemporary Issues.* Boca Raton, FL: Taylor & Francis, 2006.

Paul Campos, *The Obesity Myth: Why America's Obsession with Weight Is Hazardous to Your Health.* New York: Gotham, 2004.

Committee on Prevention of Obesity in Children and Youth et al., *Preventing Childhood Obesity: Health in the Balance.* Washington DC, National Academies, 2005.

Richard Flamenbaum, ed., *Childhood Obesity and Health Research.* New York: Nova Science, 2006.

Sander Gilman, *Fat: A Cultural History of Obesity.* Maiden, MA: Polity, 2008.

Diane Lang, *Fat Boy Chronicles.* Ann Arbor, MI: Sleeping Bear, 2010.

Taylor LeBaron, *Cutting Myself in Half.* Deerfield Beach, FL: Health Communications, 2009.

Marion Nestle, *Food Politics: How the Food Industry Influences Nutrition and Health.* Berkeley: University of California Press, 2007.

Susan Okie, *Fed Up! Winning the War Against Childhood Obesity.* Washington, DC: Joseph Henry, 2006.

Elizabeth Poskitt and Laurel Edmunds, *Management of Childhood Obesity*. New York: Cambridge University Press, 2008.

Robert Pretlow, *Overweight: What Kids Say: What's Really Causing the Childhood Obesity Epidemic*. CreateSpace, 2010.

Ellyn Satter, *Your Child's Weight: Helping Without Harming*. Madison, WI: Kelcy, 2005.

Trust for America's Health and the Robert Wood Johnson Foundation, *F as in Fat 2011: How Obesity Threatens America's Future*. Washington, DC: Trust for America's Health and the Robert Wood Johnson Foundation, July 2011.

Marissa Walsh, ed., *Does This Book Make Me Look Fat? Stories About Loving—and Loathing—Your Body*. Boston, MA: Clarion, 2008.

Periodicals and Internet Sources

Louise Knott Ahern, "Overweight Teen Just Wants to Fit in Among His Peers," *Lansing State Journal*, September 24, 2011.

David Bornstein, "Time to Revisit Food Deserts," *New York Times*, April 25, 2012.

Harriet Brown, "For Obese People, Prejudice in Plain Sight," *New York Times*, March 15, 2010.

Blair Burke, "Michelle Obama Is Your Obese Child's Cyberbully," *Wonkette*, March 21, 2011. http://wonkette.com/440945/michelle-obama-is-your-obese-childs-cyberbully.

Mahua Choudhury and Jacob E. Friedman, "Obesity: Childhood Obesity—Methylate Now, Pay Later?," *Nature Reviews Endocrinology*, August 2011.

Elena Conis, "The Waning Promise of Leptin in the Obesity Fight," *Los Angeles Times*, August 9, 2010.

Aaron Cooper, "Weight Loss Surgery Funding Cut," CNN, November 2, 2011. www.cnn.com/2011/11/02/health/obesity-surgery-cuts/index.html.

Taunya English, "African American Women and the Obesity Epidemic," Kaiser Health News, December 19, 2011. www.kaiserhealthnews.org/stories/2011/december/19/african-american-obesity.aspx.

Martinne Geller, "Soft Drink Makers Target U.S. Youth Online: Study," *Reuters*, October 31, 2011. www.reuters.com/article/2011 /11/01/us-soda-idUSTRE79U62C20111101.

Mark Goulston, "Human Cooling, Global Warming and Child-hood Obesity," *Psychology Today*, April 18, 2011.

Kate Harding, "What Michelle Obama's Childhood Obesity Project Gets Wrong," *Salon*, February 10, 2010. www.salon.com /2010/02/10/michelle_obama_weight/.

Christy Harrison, "'Time to Trim' Winners," *Slate*, March 20, 2011. http://hive.slate.com/hive/time-to-trim/article/time-to -trim-winners.

Jenna Hayes and Lorie Sicafuse, "Is Childhood Obesity a Form of Child Abuse?," *Judicature*, July/August 2010.

Phil Hayward, "Obesity on the Run," *Parks & Recreation*, July, 2010.

HealthDay, "Risk of Childhood Obesity Higher Among Minori-ties," *U.S. News & World Report*, March 1, 2010. http://health .usnews.com/health-news/family-health/childrens-health /articles/2010/03/01/risk-of-childhood-obesity-higher-among -minorities.

Melissa Healy, "Cancer Treatment Shows Promise for Rapid Weight Loss," *Los Angeles Times*, November 10, 2011.

Craig Johnson, "Are Health Ads Targeting 'Fat Kids' Too Much?," *HLNtv.com*, February 17, 2012. www.hlntv.com/article /2012/01/04/are-georgia-anti-obesity-ads-too-harsh.

David Katz, "Why We Need to Go Beyond the 'Sound Bite' for Health Information," *Huffington Post*, July 19, 2011. www.huff ingtonpost.com/david-katz-md/health-and-media_b_901440 .html.

Amina Khan, "What Is to Blame for Child Obesity?," *Los Ange-les Times*, December 21, 2009.

Lancet, "Obesity," August 26, 2011.

Anna Wilde Mathews, "Weight-Loss Surgery for Obese Teens Backed by Study," *Wall Street Journal*, February 10, 2010.

Megan McArdle, "Can Eliminating a Can of Soda a Day Keep You from Getting Fat?," *Atlantic*, October 29, 2010.

Michael Miller et al., "Triglycerides and Cardiovascular Disease," *Circulation*, April 2011.

Melissa Mitgang, "Childhood Obesity and State Intervention: An Examination of the Health Risks of Pediatric Obesity and When They Justify State Involvement," *Columbia Journal of Law and Social Problems*, Summer 2011.

Patti Neighmond, "Impact of Childhood Obesity Goes Beyond Health," NPR, July 28, 2010. www.npr.org/templates/story/story .php?storyId=128804121.

Alice Park, "Do Teen Weight Loss Programs Work Better Without Mom or Dad?," *Healthland* (blog), *Time*, February 13, 2012. http://healthland.time.com/2012/02/13/do-teen-weight-loss -programs-work-better-without-mom-or-dad.

Mandy Perryman, "Ethical Family Interventions for Childhood Obesity," *Preventing Chronic Disease: Public Health Research, Practice and Policy*, September 2011.

Peter Pollack, "The Impact of Childhood Obesity on Bones," *AAOS Now*, September 2008.

Roni Caryn Rabin, "In the Fatosphere, Big Is In, or at Least Accepted," *New York Times*, January 22, 2008.

Al Rodriguez, "Should Overweight Teen Get Gastric Bypass to Deal with Chronic Weight Problem?," ABC News, April 15, 2011. http://abcnews.go.com/WhatWouldYouDo/teen-gastric -bypass-surgery/story?id=13357390.

Rickard L. Sjöberg, Kent W. Nilsson, and Jerzy Leppert, "Obesity, Shame, and Depression in School-Aged Children: A Population-Based Study," *Pediatrics*, September 1, 2005.

Katy Waldman, "Vending Machines Affect Student Obesity?," *Slate*, January 24, 2012.

Marilyn Warm, "Foster Care for Fat Children? Gastric Bypass Surgery? Two Wrongs Call for a Fight," *SF Weekly*, July 21, 2011.

INDEX